The Rebel's Daughter

Brendan Gisby

*Too long a sacrifice
Can make a stone of the heart.
O when may it suffice?
That is Heaven's part, our part
To murmur name upon name,
As a mother names her child
When sleep at last has come
On limbs that had run wild.*

William Butler Yeats, *Easter 1916*

Copyright © 2016 Brendan Gisby
All rights reserved.
ISBN: 1534856803
ISBN-13: 978-1534856806

A McStorytellers publication

http://www.mcstorytellers.com

Contents

Foreword	4
1936: *Mother Hen*	5
1937: *Broken Hero*	10
1937: *Broken Family*	20
1938: *Orphan Life*	26
1941: *The Big House*	31
1943: *Alien Life*	37
1946: *By the Sea*	43
1948: *Derry*	49
1952: *The First Children*	56
1954: *The New House*	64
Epilogue	69
About the Author	71

Foreword

Helena Mary Bella Lane, my mother, was born into the fledgling Irish Free State, a country that was recovering from the ravages of its recent War of Independence against Britain and its more recent and even bloodier Civil War; a country that existed in a state of Purgatory between complete British Rule and complete independence from that rule.

Lena, as she was known, was also born into impoverishment. Her father, a broken war hero, preferred to wallow in drink rather than shoulder his family responsibilities. With her mother too ill to cope with the family's eight children, the twelve-year-old Lena, as the eldest daughter, became the mother hen to her brothers and sisters. But she was soon to experience the horror of her family being torn apart. When her mother was sectioned, she and her siblings were taken into care, suffering the cruel regime of clergy-run homes while they waited to be farmed out to relatives and family friends.

Lena escaped the tyranny of the nuns, only to suffer a different kind of tyranny under the guardianship of her aunt. But as soon as she was old enough, she went into domestic service, first in Ireland, then in England, and finally in Scotland, her adopted country, where she met and married my father and bore seven children of her own, six of whom are alive and kicking today.

The Rebel's Daughter is Lena's often harrowing, but ultimately triumphant, story.

Brendan Gisby
November, 2016

1936
Mother Hen

Helena Mary Bella Lane was a grand name for such a little girl, barely twelve years old, from a little house on the edge of a little village in County Leitrim in the heart of God's green island of Ireland. Of course, no-one, not even the nuns from the school down the road in Carrigallen, ever called her by that grand name. Mary and Bella were extra names she received at Holy Baptism, the former added by her mother and the latter by their parish priest, Canon O'Brian. According to her mother, Bella meant beautiful in Latin and had been added to reflect the fact she was a beautiful baby. But her father, who had little regard for the clergy, said it was a typical priest's trick to include another saint's name, a shortened form of Saint Isabella of France.

Whichever was the case, she was never called Bella. Nor Mary. And, like Saint Isabella, her first name was shortened. So she was known more plainly as Lena Lane. Not that Lena was a plain little girl; not by any manner of means. *Bella* she truly was. It was said that her mother's side of the family were of the Black Irish, descendants of Spanish immigrants to Ireland in the sixteenth century. There was no question that Lena had inherited her mother's dark Spanish looks – the hazel eyes, the sharp nose, the high cheekbones and the proud chin, but particularly the blue-black hair that cascaded in ringlets halfway down her back.

"You're Ireland's answer to Shirley Temple," her father often told her. He also often promised to take her to see a Shirley Temple film at the picture house over in Cavan Town. Until then, if such a treat was ever to materialise, she had no idea what Shirley Temple looked like. Nor did she know that the Hollywood starlet's ringlets were the product of a pair of hot curling tongs, unlike her own mass of natural, shiny, bouncing curls.

And it certainly wasn't the tune of *On the Good Ship Lollipop* that Lena was recalling this morning. As she stood on the milking stool at the big earthenware kitchen sink and washed the breakfast dishes, it was a far more sombre air she was unconsciously humming to herself.

> *"Twas down by the glenside, I met an old woman*
> *A-plucking young nettles, she ne'er saw me coming.*
> *I listened a while to the song she was humming:*
> *Glory O, Glory O, to the bold Fenian men."*

Down by the Glenside was one of the many haunting rebel songs her mother used to sing to the children when they were all gathered round the peat fire at night. But that was before she fell ill and kept to her bed for most of the time.

From the kitchen window, Lena caught sight of two of her brothers. John, who was a year older than her and the eldest child, was pretending to fire their father's rifle. Michael, who was three years her junior, was looking on in admiration.

"Father'll take a switch to your back if he catches you with his gun, John," she shouted out the open window. That gun had gone with her father through the five long years of the Black and Tan War and the Civil War that followed – or so he claimed. She knew it wasn't loaded, because a long time ago she had taken the bullets and hidden them away, more from her drunken father than her brothers. But plenty of unspent bullets could still be found all over the County. All it would take was one eejit to bring some of them to school and give them to John, and then there would be trouble.

"Put the gun back," Lena added. "And the two of yous get in here and help your wee brothers. Joseph and Brendan aren't ready for school yet, and we're running out of time."

Turning to face the window, John stood to attention, sloped the rifle across his left shoulder and gave Lena a mock salute with his right hand.

"Yes, sir, mother hen," he barked.

John had already decided he would be a soldier when he was old enough. He wouldn't be serving in the legitimate Irish Army, though. Instead, he would join the glory boys of the outlawed Irish Republican Army, like his father had done when he was a boy. There was no war to fight in these days, of course, but it had been fourteen years since Ireland had become a Free State, and the promised Republic was still nowhere in sight. With the British Government reneging again, the bold IRA needed to be on standby in the wings – or so his father kept saying.

Finished at the sink and still laughing at John's antics, Lena hopped down from the stool. While eleven-year-old Bridget and ten-year-old Margaret respectively dried and put away the dishes, she went off to check on her mother.

In addition to the combined kitchen and front room, there were two bedrooms at the rear of the tiny, single-storey house. One was used by Lena's mother and father; the other was shared by the four boys. Lena and her sisters slept in the front room, which was by far the better choice during the winter, when the peats burned through the night.

"Is there anything you need before we go, mother?" Lena asked as she entered her parents' bedroom.

Kate, her mother, was sitting up in bed as usual, her face pale and drawn, and her former raven hair now hanging grey and lank. The poor woman was still in her early thirties, but she looked twice that age. Her illness, a constant fatigue, had come on shortly after baby Elizabeth was born two years ago and seemed to grow worse week by week.

Exhausted or not, Kate could always muster a smile for Lena, her little saviour, on whom she relied more and more each day and without whom the family couldn't survive.

"Elizabeth and me are just fine, dear," she answered Lena. "Now yous get yourselves off to school. Don't be going in late and getting your knuckles rapped again by those bully nuns."

"Don't you worry, mother," Lena murmured, bending over at the top of the bed and kissing Kate lightly on the cheek.

As she straightened up, she took a peek at baby Elizabeth, who was slumbering peacefully in a cot beside the bed.

"Still no sign of your father, I suppose?" Kate asked.

Lena shook her head. "Nothing."

Kate gave out a long sigh.

"I did a washing and hung it out earlier on. It should be dry by the time we get back," Lena added and then left.

"You're such a good daughter to me," Kate sighed again in her wake.

Lena returned to the front room, expecting her siblings to be assembled there to await her inspection before they all left for school. But there was no-one to be seen. When she went outside, she understood why. The children were standing in silence, gaping up at the spectacle of Canon O'Brian astride that big dapple grey mare of his. It was as if he were a giant and they were the little people.

Like her father, Lena had little regard for priests and none at all for their accomplices, the nuns. Nor had she any time for giants on horses. She strode to the front of the line of children and stood there, arms folded.

"How are your mother and the baby?" enquired O'Brian.

"They're doing very well, Father," Lena lied defiantly. "They're both resting at the moment."

O'Brian snorted impatiently. "Look, I've no time for a visit this morning, so I'll tell you why I rode up here. Some of the parishioners – some good people of Carrigallen – are concerned that you children and your mother have been left destitute once more, what with your father, God mend his wayward soul, off on the drink again. So they petitioned me to provide you with something from the parish funds to tide you over for a bit."

He fished in a pocket, brought out a silver coin and tossed it at Lena's feet. "Take this and spend it wisely," he half-grunted.

Lena quickly picked up the coin and secreted it in her smock.

"Thank you, Father," she said.

"Now listen here, Lena," O'Brian continued. "This sort of thing can't be going on for much longer. Your father drinking and not working, and your mother sick and unable to care for her children. Mark my words, girl."

Lena looked him in the eye and stayed silent. With another snort, O'Brian wheeled the mare round and trotted away.

Lena would have dearly loved to throw the coin back at Canon O'Brian, straight between the eyes of his big, fat red face. But half-a-crown was half-a-crown and would buy a lot of food. She wouldn't spend a farthing of it, though, not until after she spoke to her mother. And right now, there was school to get to.

She looked at her brothers and sisters. Of them all, little Joseph, only six years old, was the most sensitive, the one who needed her most. She took him by the hand and set off on the two-mile trek to the village school. The others followed her. Down the hill they all trooped, mother hen and her assorted chicks.

1937
Broken Hero

It was three o'clock on a Friday afternoon in June when Jack Smith, the silver-haired landlord of Smith's Public House of Main Street, Carrigallen, emerged from his premises, pulling the door shut behind him. This was the time of day he always looked forward to, when the pub was closed for what was jokingly called the Holy Hour (although in reality it was more like two hours) and he could take a rest on the bench outside in the sun, smoking his pipe and enjoying a bit of craic with any of the lads who happened to be sitting there.

Today, though, there was only one other occupant of the bench – young Patrick Lane. Well, Jack always thought of Patrick as young, but the man must have been close to forty by then. In Jack's eyes, Patrick didn't seem to have aged since the day he and Kate, a newly married couple, came over from Arvagh to settle just outside the village more than a dozen years ago. Small and wiry, he still had that same shock of black hair and that same boyish face with its lopsided grin, although the grin hadn't been much in evidence these past two years.

According to the talk in the village, Patrick had been a leading IRA man in North Longford during the Tan War. It was also said he knew Mick Collins well. Even when he was very drunk, a frequent occurrence nowadays, Patrick never mentioned these things. And that was just as well for the sake of keeping the peace in Smith's, which was patronised by as many Anti-Treaty men as those, like Patrick, who supported the Free State.

Fifteen years after the Truce, there was still a great deal of bad blood between the two groups, not only in Carrigallen, but in every community throughout Ireland.

Patrick had left the pub a short while ago, having been in there since it opened in the morning. As usual, he had kept to himself, alone with his drink and his thoughts. The rare times he was heard speaking during all those hours was when he asked Jack for another drink. He was a carpenter to trade – and a good one at that, so Jack was told – but the only work he appeared to do now was the odd bit of labouring for the farms round about. And he probably did those jobs so he could buy more drink. Jack felt sorry for the man's poor wife and children.

"Good day to you again, Pat," he said as he sat down on the bench and began to fill his pipe. "Is that you waiting here until after the Holy Hour?"

Patrick was hunched over. He looked up at Jack for a moment, a lit cigarette dangling from his lips, the merest hint of a smile on those lips.

"It is that," he replied softly. Then he resumed staring at his boots.

Outside in the daylight, Jack could see that Patrick was unshaven and dishevelled, as if he had been sleeping rough. *Probably been doing the rounds of the pubs for days now,* he thought to himself. *And there's five of them in this wee place, with two hotels where you can get a drink to boot.*

Jack wanted to take Patrick by the shoulders, shake him hard and shout at him: *Get yourself home, man. To your bonny wife. And all your bonny children. You'll lose them otherwise. Don't be giving me any more of your money. Spend it on your family. Forget the drink. Whatever ails you, drink is not the solution.* He wanted to say all those things, but he had learned long ago never to interfere in a man's drinking business, not in this divided land. So he stayed silent and lit and pulled at his pipe instead.

The two men smoked in silence for a while. Then, out of nowhere, Patrick began to speak, although he seemed to be addressing his boots rather than Jack.

"They say that if the Brits end up going to war against that Hitler fella, De Valera will declare neutrality for the Free State. For once, I agree with the man. There's already been far too much blood spilt in this country. It's the best decision he's made in all these years."

Jack nodded and took the pipe from his mouth. "I won't argue with you there, Pat," he smiled.

And that was the end of their conversation. While Jack re-lit his pipe, Patrick returned to his thoughts – and dark and bitter thoughts they were. His mention of the man's name had reminded him how much he despised Éamon de Valera. As far as Patrick was concerned, de Valera alone was responsible for the Civil War and for Mick Collins' murder down in Cork in '22. *Mick was the greatest leader of a free Ireland that ever drew breath. And what did we get in his place, eh? De Valera. The Long Fella, all right. The long streak of putrid shite that we call our noble President. Aye, the lanky bastard's still there, strangling the life out of Ireland with his priests and his nuns.*

Angrily, Patrick threw down his cigarette dout and stamped on it. When he sat back, he closed his eyes and willed himself to remember a better time, a time before de Valera's treachery and subsequent reign. The War of Independence. 1917 to 1921. He had always regarded those years as the best of his life. They began the day he joined the IRA. It was 1917, the year after the Easter Rebellion. He was seventeen, and a smaller, skinnier and more gangling boy you couldn't have come across. After what the Brits had done to the leaders of the Rebellion, the whole country was on fire. And the fire burned brightest among the young lads like Patrick; they all wanted to fight for the cause.

On that day, Patrick travelled from Moyne, his village in North Longford, to see Seamus Brady, the Commanding Officer of the 5th Battalion. Seamus looked him up and down with those cold grey eyes of his before saying, "And how is a skinny runt of a farm-boy like you goin' to be of any help to us in the struggle? Fuck, never mind the Brits, the first strong wind that got up would blow you over."

Patrick remembered trembling with nerves and stumbling over his words until Jim McNamee, a neighbour and a second-lieutenant by that time, put in a good word for him.

"It's all right, Seamus," Jim said, "I'll vouch for young Pat here. I know his father Hugh well and his uncle Patrick. They're both good men, loyal to the cause. And this skeleton of a boy might bend with the wind, but he has some special qualities. He's a genius with his hands. Sure 'n' he built that motorcycle of his with his own hands. And he knows about guns, all types of guns."

Brady looked at Patrick with fresh eyes after that. It was the motorcycle that did it, Patrick guessed. Up there in North Longford, they needed riders who could move quickly round the countryside, delivering messages and the like between the different Companies. And they needed men who knew the countryside like the backs of their hands. Sure 'n' didn't he know every inch of the Three Corners – every inch of the country where County Longford meets County Leitrim and County Cavan?

"All right, you're in," pronounced Brady. "But don't you be letting me down, you hear?"

And that was it. He was now in the Irish Republican Army. He was a member of what became known as Moyne Company, 5th Battalion, Longford. And so began his glory years with the bold fighting men.

What followed for Patrick were exciting and dangerous times. In the first year or so, when the Army network was still being put together, his principal duty was as a rider, a messenger; him and his motorcycle travelling all over the Three Corners at all hours, delivering messages from Company to Brigade HQ and from Company to Company. That was how he met the Commander-in-chief, the great man himself, Michael Collins. Mick was up in that neck of the woods a lot in the early years, helping to organise things. Most of the time, he stayed at the Longford Arms in Granard. Patrick took many messages to him there and delivered as many for him, and they became good friends. Mick used to say to him, "You're my right-hand man up here, Pat, you know." But Patrick knew that wasn't the case. It was only Mick's way of encouraging the young fellas.

After a while, it wasn't just his motorcycle the Company wanted. There was also the business of the guns. As Jim McNamee had said on Patrick's first day, "He knows about guns, all types of guns." And so he did – how to fire them, maintain them, keep them clean and repair them. Sure 'n' what lad from a smallholding out in the country didn't know about guns? Not if he wanted to put food in the family's larder with a bit of hunting and poaching.

Next thing he was being asked to repair some guns. Then it was to clean some others and hide them. In no time at all, he was in charge of storing and maintaining the Company's whole arsenal of guns and ammunition and explosives. Not only that, but he'd become the official arms instructor – and not just for Moyne Company; for Dromard Company as well. Sure 'n' by the time he turned twenty, he was holding the rank of lieutenant colonel. And on top of all that he was the rider for both Companies, delivering messages all over the place.

For the best part of four years, he was also on duty during every single military operation by the two Companies. He had to be. It was his job to issue the guns and explosives for each engagement. And to collect them afterwards. He then needed to be there to collect and store any guns that were captured. It was exhausting work. But it was all worth it. Up in the Three Corners, it seemed like the IRA were winning the War. He was there in '20 when the 5th Battalion captured the RIC Barracks at Arvagh. And it was only months later when the bold boys of the North Longford Flying Column drove the British Army out of Ballinalee and stopped the bastards from burning down the village. Three hundred IRA men up against a force of nine hundred soldiers. What a momentous victory that was!

When he looked back now, Patrick still didn't know if he had grown too cocky by then or if he was just plain tired and wanted to get home, but one night in the Spring of '21, he slipped up badly. He was on his way to one of his arms caches to return some guns that had been used in an engagement earlier in the night. Not thinking properly, he decided against riding along one of the back lanes and took the main road instead, which was quicker.

And of course he ran straight into a bunch of Auxiliaries in an armoured car, with a truckload of Black and Tans in tow.

He was well and truly caught. With four rifles and six revolvers bundled up and strapped on the back of his motorcycle, it was red-handed at that. The Auxies and Tans were on their way down to Longford Town, and that was where they took him. The Auxies kept the guns and the Tans put him into the back of their truck. The Tans gave him a few punches and kicks to begin with, but that was all – they must have been ordered to make sure he was still in one piece for his interrogation. Sitting on the floor of the truck at the feet of those brutes, there was no shame in admitting that he wept – for himself, for what was about to pass. In all his young life, he had never felt so small and frightened and lonely.

In Longford, he was taken to the police building, where two of the Tans dragged him down the stairs, threw him headlong into one of the cells and planted another couple of hefty kicks on him. Then they left him there on his own. Nothing happened for a while. Occasionally, he could hear screams coming from the floor above. And twice he heard footsteps out in the corridor – men marching, dragging something, the back door being unlocked, a single shot ringing out. Neither time did the executed man utter a sound – no whimpering or wailing, no plea for mercy. He prayed to God that he would have their courage when it came to his turn.

Eventually, the same two Tans returned for him and took him back up the stairs to the interrogation room. All there was in the room was a wooden table with a chair at either side of it. He was pushed down into one of the chairs. Then two more men came into the room. One was a gaunt young officer, a stiff upper lip type with one of those pencil moustaches. He looked totally bored. The other could only be described as a thug. He was Scottish – from Glasgow, Patrick thought. It was said at the time that Churchill emptied Barlinnie Prison of all the thieves and rapists and murderers when he formed the Black and Tans. And this specimen was surely proof of that.

The officer sat down across the table from Patrick. He asked what

Patrick imagined were the usual questions – wanting information about him and his comrades in the IRA. And, of course, he was after knowing where Patrick was coming from and where he was going to with a bunch of guns in the middle of the night. When all Patrick told him was his name and the name of the village, the officer sighed, stood up and nodded to the thug.

"Have it your own way then, Paddy," he said.

Then he dragged his chair over to a corner of the room and lit a cigarette. He sat there smoking during the rest of the proceedings.

That's when the thug took over the interrogation. But using a pair of pliers instead of words. Having his fingernails ripped out was an experience Patrick would not wish on anyone. The pain was excruciating. And he didn't mind admitting that he squealed like a stuck pig with each nail. After the third one, he felt like he was dying. He wanted to tell them everything.

Sure 'n' wasn't it the Big Fella himself who told the men not to be martyrs if they were captured? "There's too many of you young lads getting yourselves killed during interrogation," Patrick recalled Mick saying. "All I would say is not to be stupid about it. Hold out for as long as you can, for sure. But remember your absence will be noticed by the men in your Unit, and they'll take steps to make sure they're not captured as well. So when you've had enough, go ahead and tell them. Tell them what you know. But try and mix the real information with some made-up stuff. The bastards are confused enough at the best of times; confuse them even more with some false trails. Have the fuckers running about the countryside like blue-arsed flies. But don't die into the bargain, you hear?"

Well, Patrick surprised himself and held out until all the nails on his right hand had gone. But when the thug went for the left hand, that's when he talked. He did as Mick advised. He gave some real names, but he also threw in the names of a couple of fellas who he knew were dead. It was the same with the guns. He told them the locations of some of his caches, as well as the locations of a couple of caches that didn't exist.

The officer wrote everything down in his little notebook and left the room. And then the thug started on Patrick's left hand. You see, it didn't matter to him. None of it fucking mattered. The sadistic bastard was always going to have his way whatever happened.

After it was over, after the thug was finished, the Tans dragged Patrick downstairs and put him back in the cell. He really did want to die then. It wasn't just the pain, though that was awful enough. It was the shame as well. No matter that Mick had told the men to do it if they were tortured, it was the shame of having betrayed the men in his Company.

So he lay there in the cell, praying for them to come soon and take him out the back and shoot him like he had heard with the others. But it seemed like days passed and nothing happened. And when they did come, Jesus wept, it was for to release him. He still didn't know to that day why he was released. Maybe it was because the Truce was about to be declared and the Tans had received orders to unload their prisoners. Or maybe they just wanted to cause trouble, making Patrick out to be some kind of traitor. If it was the latter reason, it certainly worked in some quarters.

Before they finally let him go, the Tans had a little surprise up their sleeves – a sort of parting gift. A group of them drove him into Moyne. They got out at the start of the village, where they tied a big Union Jack round him. Then they made him march along Main Street, with them following and one of the galoots beating a drum so as to attract everybody's attention. Aside from the torture, Patrick hadn't eaten or drunk anything since being captured, so he was very weak and he stumbled rather than marched. He fell a couple of times, but a few dunts from their rifle butts on his back and shoulders had him up again soon enough. Then, when they got to the other end of the street, they just left him there, still wrapped in the Union Jack. He was on his knees and crying in front of the whole village. The final humiliation.

His mother and father came for him and took him home. And that's where he stayed hidden away and recovering for weeks, months. By that time, the Truce was in force and the War, for him at least, was over. But only for another one – the Civil War – to start up. He was on Michael Collins' side, of course, a Free Stater, but he didn't have the stomach to get involved in the fighting, going up against his own countrymen, many of them good friends from the 5th Battalion.

Thankfully, the fighting didn't last long. The Staters came out on top and Ireland became a free country of sorts, but with de Valera as President and not the Big Fella. The fucking irony of it!

When things settled down after the Civil War, Patrick tried to get on with his life in Moyne. But it was impossible. There were fingers constantly pointing at him. The two men who were murdered back at that gaol in Longford happened to come from the village. It was no coincidence that he had been caught as well. They had all been returning from the same engagement that night. They had all been betrayed. Unfortunately, the families of the two men were convinced Patrick was the traitor. He knew that the men were captured long before he was, but there was no talking to those people. They just wouldn't listen. He had to get out of there, so he left to stay with a relative over in Arvagh. He was twenty-three by then and needed to start his life again.

And so he did. It wasn't long before he had met the dark and sultry Kate, one of the proud Kiernans of County Cavan. Nor was it long before he and Kate had married and set up house in Carrigallen. Then the children came, nine of them in all; a whole clan of beautiful, raven-haired children. Tragically, poor wee Catherine didn't survive past her second year, but the latest baby, little Elizabeth, made up for her loss.

For a while, they all had a good life, with him doing a job as a carpenter, working with his hands again. But as the years passed, he became restless. There was something not right, something eating at him. It took him a long time to realise it was the country itself that wasn't right. It seemed that the whole of Ireland – with a lot of help from de Valera, of course – just wanted to forget everything that had happened since the Rising in '16. He could understand why people would want to erase the Civil War from their memories. But not the War of Independence. Not all the deaths and sacrifices and suffering that were involved. Surely not that.

Then a couple of years back he became so depressed about the whole matter that he took to the drink, only doing enough work to keep a roof over the heads of Kate and the children – and to keep himself in whiskey, of course. Otherwise, he neglected his family and left them to fend for themselves. To make matters worse, Kate fell ill. According to the doctor, O'Reilly, who lived just a few houses along from Smith's, the illness was more mental than physical and was probably caused by the stress of having all those mouths to feed with no money coming in. Which only served to make Patrick want to drink more and stay away longer.

And so here I am, he muttered to himself. *Me and my sorry arse waiting for the bar to open again, while my wife and kids go hungry.*

In one of those blindingly sober moments that drunk men often experience, Patrick was suddenly full of the deepest remorse. There were tears streaming down his face. He was such a poor husband to Kate. And such a poor father to his children. It was true that he had fought for his country's freedom and suffered as a result. It was also true that his ungrateful country had betrayed him. But that was no reason for him to betray his family, to make them suffer. It wasn't fair at all. He should put an end to this madness right now. He should get himself home to become a proper husband and father again. Wiping away his tears with both hands, he stood up, swayed for a moment and then moved off unsteadily without saying a word.

Jack Smith watched Patrick half-stagger and half-march along Main Street on his way out of the village. Not for the first time, he was pleased to be losing a customer. It was almost as if Patrick had heard and heeded his unspoken advice. Lighting his pipe again and smiling, he wondered playfully if it had been an example of that mental telepathy business he had read about. Then he laughed. It would surely be declared a miracle if he told Canon O'Brian about it. And no doubt the bold Canon would have folk flocking to Carrigallen to pray at the site of the miracle, the Holy Bench itself.

1937

Broken Family

When their repentant father set off from Smith's on that Friday afternoon, resolved to be a better and more sober man, Lena and the rest of the children were already well on their way home from school. As usual, Lena held Joseph's hand as they walked up the hill. As usual, too, the others dawdled at some distance behind.

Joyful that school was over for another week, Lena hummed a happy tune to herself. It wasn't so much the school that she disliked, but more the nuns who ran it. There wasn't a drop of humour in those hard-faced harridans. And they seemed to spend less time teaching and more meting out punishments – with rulers and leather straps and whatever else came to hand. So long as you knew your Catechism off by heart, they didn't care how good you were at reading and writing and arithmetic. But get a word wrong in Catechism, or forget a word, and it's as if you've committed a mortal sin and the wrath of Heaven will be visited upon you. If she had the choice, the only reason Lena would go to school at all was for the Gaelic lessons, which were given by little Sister Bernadette, who was slightly more human than any of her colleagues.

But Lena consoled herself with the thought that when she turned fourteen the following year she would be rid of the school and its nuns for ever. Then she would be able to work and start earning some much-needed money for the family. Perhaps she would take a job at the big house down in the village. It was said that Lord Kilbracken was always looking to employ scullery maids and the like. Her father wouldn't like it. She could hear him now. "I won't have a daughter of mine working for the English," he'd declare during one of his drunken rants. Anyway, he wasn't likely to be around to either approve or disapprove.

Before any of that, though, it would be her brother John's turn to get a job. He was fourteen now and was due to leave school after the summer. Lena hoped he would be able to find some farm work quickly and not, as he was threatening to do, run off into the hills to join the IRA. Putting food on the table was much more important than marching with guns and pretending to kill Orangemen from the North. To make matters worse, Michael, who hero-worshipped John, was also threatening to follow his older brother.

The IRA nonsense was their father's fault, of course; he was forever encouraging the boys to take up arms as soon as they were old enough. In fact, everything was their father's fault – or so Lena had decided a long time ago. Father was to blame for them feeling hungry all the time. Not that they were truly starving. They ate potatoes and other vegetables they grew themselves. They kept chickens for their eggs. And there was milk (and sometimes cheese) from their nanny goat, Dev, so-called by father "because that ould beast is as mean-tempered and contrary as our noble President". But what they had was never enough. Nor was there ever any meat, unless they were forced to kill one of their precious chickens.

Father was also to blame for the state of their feet. All the girls' shoes and the boys' boots were falling apart, but there was no money to replace them or even repair them. Nowadays, they were only worn for Mass on Sundays. The rest of the time, the children went barefoot. Which was fine during the summer, but an altogether different matter when there was frost or snow on the ground.

Much worse than their hunger and their bare feet, though, was the condition of their mother, which Lena blamed entirely on her father's negligence. The poor woman was able to do less for herself these days and even less for baby Elizabeth, so much so that Lena, Bridget and Margaret had been taking turns to stay off school to help her – thus incurring the wrath of the harridans. Their mother had also taken to talking to herself constantly. The only time she came to life and seemed to return to her old self was when father made one of his rare visits to lay some money on the kitchen table. Then she would believe that everything was going to be fine again, that the family would be whole again. But it was never long before her hopes were crushed by her cruel and heartless husband sneaking back down to the village to resume his drinking.

So much anger had welled up in Lena as she thought of her father that she came to a sudden halt and spat on the ground.

Little Joseph looked up at her with big, concerned eyes. "Are you all right there, Lena?" he asked.

Only then did Lena realise that she and Joseph had reached the top of the hill, from where they had a full view of their house and its front yard a short distance away. And only then did she become aware of the commotion outside the house.

"No, I'm not, Joseph," she answered her brother, automatically tightening her grip on his hand.

At first sight, it seemed to Lena that an army had invaded their home. Parked on the road alongside the yard were three identical-looking black motorcars. The nearest one belonged to Doctor O'Reilly, who at that moment was leading their clearly distraught mother across the yard towards it. With a shawl wrapped tightly around her hunched shoulders, she was weeping, babbling to herself and staring at the ground, as if she was afraid to look elsewhere.

Also in the yard were two nuns, neither of whom Lena had seen before. One was cradling Elizabeth in her arms in an effort to placate the upset toddler. The other carried a suitcase in each hand. Lena recognised the green cardboard cases that were usually kept on top of the wardrobe in her parents' bedroom. This latter nun was walking towards the motorcars parked behind Doctor O'Reilly's, where the familiar figures of Canon O'Brian and his assistant, Father Dolan, stood watching the proceedings.

By this time, the rest of their brothers and sisters had caught up with Lena and Joseph. All seven gaped at the scene for some moments. Then Lena, still clutching Joseph's hand, marched in the direction of the priests. The others followed close behind them.

Father Dolan was first to see the children. Tall and very thin, he walked towards them, wringing his hands, as was his wont, and looking very nervous. "That young fella's not cut out for the priesthood – he's far too polite and timid," their father once said of him.

"What are yous doing with my mother? And the baby?" Lena demanded even before Father Dolan reached her, the defiant tone of her voice making him more nervous.

"I'm – I'm so sorry. There's been an incident. A terrible incid–" he began, his long neck arching down closer to Lena, but he was cut short by the thicker set Canon O'Brian stepping in front of him.

"Yes, there's been a terrible incident," boomed the latter. "But for God's grace and the quick thinking of young Father Dolan here, it would have been much more terrible. Earlier today, the good Father happened to be driving past Carrigallen Lough after visiting a parishioner along there when he caught sight of your mother up to her waist in the water and holding the baby in her arms. The demented woman was threatening to drown both herself and the baby. She kept saying there was no point in going on. But Father Dolan spent an hour talking to her and persuaded her to come out of the water. Then he drove her and the baby down to Doctor O'Reilly so that he could check them over."

O'Brian paused there and looked at his assistant for confirmation of the events he had just related. Still wringing his hands, the lanky priest started to say something, thought better of it and simply nodded his agreement. Meanwhile, Lena and her siblings stood in silence, too shocked to say anything.

"Now, children," O'Brian resumed, "I want you to listen carefully to what I have to say. And don't any one of you be doing anything stupid, you hear?"

He paused again, this time to look directly down at Lena, who remained silent, with the same defiant expression on her face.

"The good doctor and I have sectioned your mother. Do any of you understand what that means? It means that she'll go to live in a mental hospital for a while – until she's better, that is. It's for her own good, you understand, for her own safety."

There was still no reaction from the children.

"Now, with your poor mother away and your sinful father not around, we can't be leaving you boys and girls on your own, do you understand? It's against the law, apart from anything else. We'll be looking to find families – relatives, we hope – who'll be willing to take you in. But for the time being we're going to have to place you in care. The boys will come with Father Dolan and I to a home for orphan boys not far from here. The girls, including the baby, will go with the two Sisters here to a separate home, also not far away. The good Sisters have already packed all your clothes for you."

It was only then that Lena reacted, the defiance in her voice now replaced by a pleading tone. "No!" she cried, tears streaming down her face. "Please, no. Please don't split us up. We're a family. I can look after all of them."

"I'm afraid that's not possible," O'Brian replied curtly. "Or lawful," he added.

Then he took hold of Joseph's free hand and tried to pull the youngster away from Lena. "Come along now, boy. And you other lads," he ordered. "You all come with me and Father Dolan in his motorcar."

Small as he was, Joseph stood his ground and clutched Lena's hand even tighter. Then he, too, erupted in tears. His wailing was so loud it caused O'Brian to let go of his hand, whereupon Lena knelt down and wrapped both her arms around him.

"I need you to be brave for me, Joseph," she said, trying hard to stifle her own weeping. "I need you to go with your brothers. It'll only be for a short while. Then we'll all be back together again. I promise."

"Are you sure now, Lena?" Joseph asked between loud sobs. "All right, but only if you're sure."

"I am," whispered Lena, giving him one last hug.

Then she stood up and watched as her four brothers, led by John, walked towards the open rear door of the middle motorcar, where Father Dolan stood holding one of the green suitcases. Still crying, she in turn led Bridget and Margaret to the third car, where one of the nuns ushered them into the back seat, shoving in the second suitcase after them.

The motorcars moved off in a convoy, heading back down the hill and onward to their respective destinations. Save for the occasional sob from Joseph, there was silence in the car carrying the boys. Father Dolan looked sorrowful as he drove, while Canon O'Brian sat stone-faced beside him. Behind them, John also sat stone-faced and seething with emotions. He was anxious about this "home for orphan boys" they were being driven to. He was angry with the way in which his family had been torn apart. Above all, though, he felt ashamed. He was the eldest. He should have done something to protect the family. He should have fought back. But instead he meekly followed the priests' orders.

All was quiet as well in the last car. Even baby Elizabeth, still in the arms of the nun in the passenger seat, had settled down for the time being. Like John, Lena was also full of emotions, but the overwhelming one in her case was that of hatred – hatred for the man who had caused all this. Sitting at the right-hand rear window, she glanced back at their little house. Unperturbed by the catastrophe that had just taken place, the chickens were still pecking in the yard. But Dev, the goat, was nowhere to be seen, probably having fled when the visitors arrived. Then she caught sight of him. Her father was standing by the side of the road at the top of the hill, watching as the convoy sped away from him. He seemed lost and perplexed. He recognised Lena. He saw the look she gave him. That withering look. It would stay with him for the rest of his troubled life.

1938
Orphan Life

Standing on a stool and bending over the rim of the huge, galvanised tin cylinder that served as a washtub, Lena used a pair of wooden tongs to churn the tub's contents. Her face and the ringlets across her forehead were wet from the steam rising from the murky water. The work reminded her of the times she would do the family's washing back home in Carrigallen. Except that here in Our Lady of Succour Industrial School the washtub was much bigger and the clothes in it were nuns' habits. The habits belonged to the Sisters of Mercy who ran the school and who lived in the adjoining convent.

Not that much schooling ever went on in the place. It was more of a workhouse than a school. All the girls – and there were hundreds of them – were set "chores" by the nuns. Lena's main chore was to help in the laundry room. She was also responsible for making sure that little Elizabeth was washed, dressed and fed daily. Elizabeth was kept in what was laughably called the "nursery", but which was really a big room in which the toddlers were locked during the day. They could scream the place down and tear each other apart in there for all that the nuns seemed to care.

Lena's other sisters, Bridget and Margaret, spent most of their time working in the kitchens. There was also work to be had outside in the gardens, which Lena would have much preferred to do, but gardening chores were usually assigned to the older girls, the ones who had spent all or most of their lives at the school; some of them were even grown women. And that was Lena's biggest fear: that the Lane girls would live their whole lives in the place. They had been there for almost a year now, with no word of anyone coming to collect them. And Lena had given up asking the nuns when anyone was going to come. It wasn't so much because they never answered her, but more because of the slaps across the face they gave her instead for her so-called "insolence". It had been the same at the beginning whenever she asked how her mother was doing and what was happening to her brothers. So she had learned quite early on to keep her mouth closed, to get on with her work and to watch out for her sisters as best she could.

The school was in the village of Newtownforbes in County Longford. It was less than thirty miles from her little house in County Leitrim, but as far as Lena was concerned it might as well have been on another continent. It was run like a prison, from which few were ever allowed out. And the nuns were like prison warders, forcing the girls to wash and cook and clean for them so that they could strut about looking all holy and high and mighty, while saying their prayers and professing their love of God.

Those nuns. The Sisters of No Mercy, the girls called them. If Lena thought the ones at the school in Carrigallen had been harsh, this lot were a hundred times worse. Everything and nothing could at any moment provoke a swipe from them with a stick or a strap or whatever was in their hands. If not that, it would be a slap, a punch or even a kick. Making eye contact with any of them was considered insolent, so the girls had to look at the floor whenever they came near.

It would have to be the case, of course, that the worst of the nuns, the biggest bully of them all, happened to be the one in charge of the laundry room. Lena was convinced that Sister Agatha was a man in disguise. She was big and heavy like a man. She walked with her legs wide apart like a man. She hit out like a man with that cane she carried wherever she went. And she had a moustache. If she wasn't a man, she was certainly the ugliest woman Lena had ever seen. She was also Lena's nemesis. "I do not like pretty little girls," she once warned her, after which she regularly threatened to shave off Lena's beautiful hair. Having seen her do exactly that to a couple of the Dublin girls who had annoyed her, Lena knew it was no idle threat, so she stayed out of Sister Agatha's way as much as was possible.

The majority of the girls at the school were from Dublin, orphans for the most part, who had been sent there by the Courts after being caught stealing or begging. They were a rough crowd who cursed a lot, using swearwords Lena had never heard before. In the early days, when they quizzed her about her background, Lena had decided that she and her sisters would also claim to be orphans and hence save themselves from being ridiculed for having a drunken father and a mad mother. With their father away, their mother incarcerated and no-one coming for them, they were no better than orphans anyway.

When the Dublin girls found out that Lena's brothers had also been put in a home, what they said about the priests who ran the homes being as bad as the Sisters of Mercy had Lena concerned for the boys, particularly the bit about how some of the priests might be interfering with them. Although she didn't fully understand what "interfering" meant, it had her worried, not so much about John and Michael, who were tough like their father, or even Brendan, who had the same spirit as his older brothers, but mostly about Joseph. She knew that Joseph just didn't have it in him to fight back. And she couldn't bear to think about him being bullied or worse day and night by someone like Sister Agatha.

Think of the devil and she's sure to appear, Lena muttered to herself when she spotted Sister Agatha at the door of the laundry room. She bent closer to the water, as if to hide from the nun, but it was no use – Sister Agatha marched straight to the washtub, swinging her cane with one hand and holding a cloth bag in the other.

"You, girl," she growled at Lena, "get down from there and come with me. The Mother Superior wants to speak to you."

Lena hopped down from the stool and walked to the adjacent wall, where she stood on her tiptoes to hang the tongs on their hook. Then she wiped her wet hands on her smock.

"Hurry, girl!" Sister Agatha shouted before turning on her heel and striding out of the room.

Lena had to half-run behind the nun to keep up with her. They headed out of the school, but stopped at a small door to the side of the main entrance. Sister Agatha opened the door, ushered Lena through it, closed it behind her and set off again at a fast pace. Lena knew the door led into the convent, which the girls were forbidden to enter. As she scuttled along a series of dark corridors into the belly of the building, her mind was in a turmoil. Why on earth would the Mother Superior want to see her? Was she to be punished for something she had done? Or something she had omitted to do? Or had something terrible happened to one of her sisters? *Not baby Elizabeth, please!* Or perhaps it was news about her mother. Had she gotten worse? Had she died? Lena prayed the visit was for punishment and not for any of those other things.

When at last they came to a halt outside an arched, oak-panelled door, Sister Agatha knocked on the door, opened it and motioned to Lena to go through. Then she, too, entered the room to stand a few paces behind Lena, as if to bar any attempted escape by the little girl.

"This is Lena Lane, Reverend Mother," she addressed the tiny figure sitting behind a large, ornate desk, its head bent over some papers and its face completely hidden by a nun's veil that was several sizes too big.

For what seemed like an eternity to Lena, the figure did not move. When it finally looked up from the papers, it was to reveal the face of a wrinkled, old woman, a face that reminded Lena of a withered apple, and a pair of eyes that were small, brittle-blue and cold.

"Well now, Lena Lane," the Mother Superior said in a surprisingly loud and shrill voice for such a small person, "it appears that you'll be leaving us today. I hope your time at Our Lady of Succour has been instructive and that you will go out into the world a better and more devout person. Your Aunt—"

She paused to examine one of the papers, looked up again and continued.

"Yes, your Aunt Bridget is waiting at reception to collect you. Sister Agatha has already put your belongings together. Off you go with her now.

And may God go with you."

Just the sight of the Mother Superior's face and the sound of her voice had Lena crying. She still hadn't taken in what the old woman told her when Sister Agatha thrust the cloth bag into her hands. Then she realised the worst. It was only her that was going. She would be leaving the others behind, unprotected from these monsters.

"But what about my sis–" she tried to ask through her tears.

Before she could finish the sentence, Sister Agatha had hauled her by the arm out of the room and was now marching her along another dark corridor, this time in the direction of the convent's main entrance.

May God go with you. The Mother Superior's last words were still ringing in Lena's ears. *But what kind of God would let these terrible things happen?* she asked herself. *What kind of God would allow a family to be torn apart twice inside a year? There can't be a God if that's the case. He doesn't exist.*

As they approached the reception area, Lena recognised the lady standing there as her Aunt Bridget. She was a stern-looking woman, wearing her Sunday-best coat and hat and holding a large handbag. Like her brother, Lena's father, she had thick black hair, a prominent nose and bushy eyebrows. Lena took longer to recognise the person standing next to her. It had been less than a year, but he looked much taller and more manly than when she last saw him. Her tears stopped and a grin broke out on her face. *Perhaps there is a God, after all,* she thought as she rushed to hug her brother John.

1941

The Big House

Just as Aunt Bridget had taught her, Lena walked sedately with her back straight while she carried the silver tray up from the kitchens and through to the drawing room of Castle Forbes. It wasn't really a castle, of course, but a large country mansion built to resemble a castle, with towers and turrets and battlements and the like. Although she had been in service there for nearly a year now, Lena still hadn't fully taken in the grandeur and opulence of the place. Nor had she yet gotten over the fact that the entrance to the Castle Forbes estate was slap-bang in the centre of Newtownforbes village, only a short walk from the so-called Industrial School of Our Lady of Succour and an even shorter walk from Aunt Bridget's house, which sat on the edge of the estate and was owned by it. *Ireland is a small place*, someone once told Lena, and that surely was the case.

Aunt Bridget's house was more of a smallholding than anything else, with cows and chickens and a large garden, all of which had to be tended in order to supply the kitchens of Castle Forbes with milk, eggs, potatoes and other vegetables. Aunt Bridget hadn't always lived there. Her tenancy of the place only began in 1938, when, having decided to become the guardian of the two eldest children of her brother Patrick, she agreed with the estate owners, the Earl and Countess of Granard, that she and her new wards would take over and do everything needed to manage the smallholding on behalf of the estate. As part of that arrangement, she also agreed to give up her job as lady's maid to Countess Granard, a position that had required her to reside at Castle Forbes and to accompany the American-born millionairess on her frequent trips to London and Paris, as well as on Her Ladyship's occasional visits to the New York home of her father, the magnate Ogden Mills. With the threat of War in Europe looming closer every day, those trips had been put on hold, resulting in Bridget's services rarely being required. Overall, therefore, the arrangement was of mutual benefit.

Not that either John or Lena regarded any part of the arrangement as beneficial to them. Not at first, anyway. It was true that Aunt Bridget had rescued both of them from the homes they had been put into – and Lena, in particular, from the clutches of the ogre that was Sister Agatha – but they discovered soon enough that they had simply swapped one harsh regime for another. Their so-called saviour had them working every day from first light till darkness fell. And each day was an endless round of milking, feeding, mucking out, digging and weeding. Aunt Bridget, they found, was a severe woman who rarely showed them any affection and who never cracked a smile. She was also very devout, making them accompany her to Mass on Sundays and Holidays of Obligation, and insisting that they said the rosary at night before they went to bed.

Gradually, though, they came to realise that their aunt was actually a good-hearted person. After all, hadn't she, a spinster in her thirties, given up a comfortable and highly respected position at the Big House to look after them? No-one had forced her to do that. And hadn't the running of the smallholding been her idea, a way to provide a roof over their heads? Gradually, too, they came to understand that if she was overly severe, it was because she was driven, desperate to ensure that the smallholding worked. Which it did after a while. Then, when she relaxed a little, their work regime eased somewhat and they caught the odd smile escaping her normally pursed lips.

The pair of them warmed to her even more when they learned that all along she had been attempting to persuade other members and friends of the Lane family to house the rest of Patrick's children. Then, about a year after they began living at the smallholding, she became their friend for life when, through her persistent efforts, the Higgins family agreed to take in both Michael and Brendan. The Higgins were old neighbours of Bridget's parents who ran a farm up by Aughnacliffe way. And the school they sent the two boys to was close enough for Michael to make regular bicycle trips down to Castle Forbes during lunchtime so that he could visit Lena. To be sure, Ireland really was a small place.

While Lena was overjoyed when she was told that her two brothers would be looked after by people whom Aunt Bridget described as "good country folk", she was also very concerned that Joseph would be left on his own in the hands of the priests. But John, who never spoke about his time in the boys' home, reassured her that Joseph was "being cared for". Later, Michael was to confirm John's statement and to elaborate on it by telling her that a young priest, having recognised Joseph's sensitivity, had taken him under his wing; there was even talk of Joseph perhaps going into the priesthood himself one day. After hearing that, Lena worried less about Joseph and only hoped that his mentor was kindly and understanding like young Father Dolan back home in Carrigallen.

Which left Lena to worry about her three sisters still at the Industrial School along the road. Again, though, she was reassured of their wellbeing, this time by her aunt who apparently received regular updates on them from one of the School's nuns whom she had befriended. Bridget and Margaret, it seemed, had stepped into Lena's shoes and were both looking after little Elizabeth. And Bridget, in particular, was getting on famously as a cook in the School's kitchens.

By the time they entered their second year living with Aunt Bridget, John and Lena were fast approaching adulthood, so it was not surprising that they should begin to think about their future lives outside of that place. Their lighter workload also by that time helped them see what might be possible. Although he continued with his work at the smallholding, John joined the local Unit of the IRA, just as he had threatened to do when he was younger. Lena didn't blame him this time, and even Aunt Bridget turned a blind eye. The Irish Free State was under threat. De Valera's declaration of the country's neutrality at the outset of the War had angered the British. The hard men up in Ulster were particularly incensed. There was constant talk, fuelled by the latter, of a full-scale invasion by the British Army in order to secure the strategic ports along the west coast. The legitimate Irish Army had gone on alert. Their outlawed IRA counterparts had done likewise.

As for Lena, her thoughts at that time were less concerned with Britain's War with Germany and more with matters closer to home. She had her sites set firmly on taking a job up at the Big House. And for months she pleaded with, pestered and cajoled Aunt Bridget about the job until the woman gave in and promised to try to find her one at Castle Forbes, but only after she turned sixteen. In the meantime, Aunt Bridget would instruct Lena in how to deport herself as a servant to the Earl and Countess and their four grown-up children.

Aunt Bridget was true to her word. Not only did she secure a position for Lena, but she also used her influence to ensure that her niece would not be required to start at the bottom of the servants' heap. At the age of sixteen, Lena entered Castle Forbes as a trained parlour-maid. And there she was today, almost a year later, in her black uniform with its white neck and cuffs, confidently delivering Her Ladyship's midmorning coffee.

As she passed Oliver, the footman standing in the entrance hall, Lena smiled demurely at him. Oliver had a "thing" for Lena, as had all the other young male servants in the house, not to mention a dozen or more young men down in the village. And who would blame any of them? Small, slim and dark, Lena had developed into a beautiful teenage Irish rose. Gone were the tight ringlets of her childhood, to be replaced by lustrous waves of blue-black hair that bounced and shimmered as she walked. The fact that she was well aware of her attractiveness added to the confidence of her gait. In the full knowledge also that Oliver would be gazing at her back, she produced an extra little flounce in her step as she entered the drawing room.

Her back propped up by any number of cushions, Beatrice Forbes *née* Mills, the Countess of Granard, was stretched out on an enormous white sofa, reading a book. It was said that in her younger years she was a striking-looking woman, and even now, as she approached her sixtieth birthday, she retained some of that beauty. Across the room, her husband, Bernard, the 8th Earl of Granard, sat in a large Moroccan leather armchair and studied *The Times* of London, which, in spite of the War, was still shipped over to him regularly. A tall, thin man, somewhat older than the Countess, he was a member of the Anglo-Irish nobility, now retired from a career in Irish politics and before that a military career in the British Army.

It didn't escape Lena's notice that the comfort in which this couple and their offspring lived was in glaring contrast to life outside Castle Forbes. With imports of coal, oil and wheat from Britain having all but dried up because of the War, an Emergency had been declared in Ireland. Severe rationing was in force. People were hungry. Some were starving. Typhus had reappeared in certain quarters. By all accounts, the whole country was in a poor state. Yet there was no evidence of any hardships being felt in the sumptuousness of the Forbes' drawing room. There was even place for luxuries like the Cuban cigar the Earl was smoking and the coffee in the silver pot on the silver tray that Lena was now setting down on a small Queen Anne table within arm's reach of the reclining Countess.

"Your coffee, Your Ladyship," Lena said softly as she stepped back from the table.

"Thank you, Lena," acknowledged the Countess without taking her eyes from her book. Then she waved a hand fleetingly to signify that Lena was dismissed.

Lena stepped further back and performed the minutest of curtsies. As she turned to leave, the Earl noisily put down his newspaper, pulled the cigar from his mouth and cleared his throat.

"You, girl," he beckoned to Lena. "Um, yes, you–"

"Lena," the Countess interjected impatiently, still without drawing her eyes away from the book.

"Ah, yes, of course."

Lena curtsied properly this time. "Your Lordship?" she smiled.

"Yes, young Lena, I've been meaning to have a word with you. My good friend, Harry Primrose, the Earl of Rosebery, over in England has asked for my help with... um... a bit of a problem he's experiencing because of this blasted War. He owns a very large house, Mentmore Towers, which is much larger than this one, and he needs lots of... um... staff to look after it. But it seems that a good number of his male staff have left him to enlist in the Forces and that practically all the younger women have gone off to work in munitions factories and such like to help in the War effort. Dashed inconvenient for him, don't you think so?"

Lena didn't understand what any of this had to do with her. She simply nodded and kept smiling.

"Anyway, poor Harry is now looking elsewhere to... um... replenish the staff. There's an embargo at the moment on workers from Ireland travelling to Britain, but he's been tipped the wink that the embargo will be lifted shortly. Which is where I come in. I already have a number of people from here and other estates lined up, all ready to go over and work at Mentmore. I'm wondering if you would like to join them. You're very efficient and... um... presentable. You'd be an asset to the place. And, of course, it would be an excellent opportunity should you wish to pursue a career in... um... domestic service, like your aunt did. Well, what do you think, my dear?"

Gone was Lena's smile – and her composure. She stood with her mouth open, speechless.

The Earl laughed. "I'm sorry I've sprung this on you. You don't have to give me an answer immediately. Go and speak to your aunt um–"

"Bridget," the Countess interjected again, just as impatiently.

"Yes, go and speak to Bridget and let me know what you two decide."

"Thank you, Your Lordship," Lena gushed, curtseying again and again as she backed out of the room, almost knocking over the furniture.

Out in the hall, she gave a confused Oliver a dazzling smile. *A career in domestic service.* Those words were still ringing in her ears.

1943
Alien Life

It was very early on a bitter midwinter morning at Mentmore Towers, the Buckinghamshire seat of the 6th Earl of Rosebery, set in the heart of England's green and pleasant land, when Lena took her place at the long wooden table in the servants' hall for the first breakfast sitting. Because of the large number of servants employed by the house – Lena estimated there were well over one hundred – three sittings had to be held each morning. As befitted her age and rank, Lena sat with the other young housemaids at the bottom end of the table. At the table's head was Chadwick, the butler, flanked on one side by Grace, the housekeeper (who was also Chadwick's wife), and on the other by Mrs Maillard, the cook.

Only the Earl and Countess of Rosebery and their teenage son, Neil, whose official title was Lord Primrose, addressed Chadwick by his proper name. To everyone else, including all his staff, he was known as Chaddie. He was a small, dapper, pleasant man who spoke with an Estuary twang. Grace was taller and thinner than him, with a more refined bearing and voice. While they may have given the impression of an odd couple, there was little doubt that they were devoted to each another. And together they strove to run a happy crew at Mentmore Towers.

With more than thirty members of that crew now assembled for breakfast, understandably the servants' hall was a noisy place. Much clattering of cutlery and crockery was accompanied by much chattering. At the top end of the table, the main topic of discussion was, as ever, the latest news of the War. The discussion was upbeat for a change. It seemed that the Germans were on the run in North Africa, in Russia and throughout Europe. Perhaps there was an end in sight after all this time.

But it was the unusually harsh winter weather for the area that dominated the talk further down the table. An arctic wind had been blasting from the east for several days, turning the snow that covered the extensive grounds of the house into sheets of ice. As often occurs when many people are speaking at the same time, there was a sudden lull in the conversation, during which Lena's one and only contribution to the weather debate was heard clearly by the whole company.

"Sure 'n' that wind could freeze the balls off a brass monkey," she declared in her unmistakable brogue.

Her statement was met with an audible intake of breath and then silence. Lena's eyes darted round the table from one impassive face to the next. She looked worried and perplexed.

"I'm sorry, did I say something wrong?" she asked. "I was only repeating what one of the gardeners said to me yesterday. I thought he was talking about a weathervane or something."

In response to which the room erupted in roars of laughter, with even Chaddie and Grace joining in. But a few moments later, Chaddie had to bring the merriment to an end.

"Quiet now, quiet now!" he shouted, standing up and pointing to the ceiling. "We don't want Her Ladyship coming down here to investigate and causing a fuss, now do we? Let's finish our breakfast quietly, please, after which I have an important announcement to make."

Before he took his seat again, he looked down the table directly at Lena. "And as for you, young Mary, I think it's high time Grace and I took you to one side and explained some of the more... erm... colourful terms used hereabouts, terms an innocent Irish country girl like yourself won't have heard before."

Red-faced, Lena nodded at Chaddie. Then she smiled serenely for the benefit of the rest of the company to indicate that the embarrassment was of no consequence to her. The truth was that she didn't mind being laughed at for her little *faux pas*. As Chaddie had said, she was an innocent abroad. And there was never any malice in the laughter. In fact, everyone she had met since arriving at Mentmore Towers the year before had been very kind to her, particularly Chaddie and Grace, who had immediately taken her under their wing and treated her as if she was the daughter they never had. Nor had a single person cast up to her the fact that Ireland had kept out of the War. Besides, there were plenty of other Irish people at Mentmore Towers, many of whom had come over on the boat with her, having also been recruited by friends of Lord Rosebery in the nobility.

The only sour note in her experience of England so far was having the word ALIEN stamped in big capital letters across her visa. That and being required to report at the police station in Mentmore every week. Still, the recent weather aside, the walk down through the grounds to the village was usually a pleasant one and reminded her a lot of the countryside she came from. But it had been a fair old rigmarole to obtain her visa in the first place, what with papers having to go back and forward between London and Dublin – and in the middle of wartime, too. And she may not have obtained the visa at all without her aunt's help when she was filling in the application.

"Now, Lena," Aunt Bridget had advised, "don't be complicating matters by putting down details of your father and mother. That wouldn't be wise, particularly given Patrick's past activities in the IRA. Just claim that both your parents are dead and give them nothing to be checking up on. As you well know, that's a common situation here in Ireland, especially now when starvation and disease are blighting the land again."

So there she was today, little orphan Lena, an alien in a foreign country. Except her name wasn't Lena any more, at least not while she worked at Mentmore Towers. There was already a Lena among the domestic staff when she first arrived, so Chaddie decided that to avoid any confusion she should be called by her second name. She didn't mind at all. And Mary was also her mother's first name. But even now, many months later, she still wasn't completely used to the change.

Nor had nineteen-year-old Mary (formerly known as Lena) fully gotten used to Mentmore Towers. Nothing anyone could have said beforehand would have prepared her for its sheer size and grandeur. Castle Forbes was a plain little country house by comparison. She reckoned it would take a person years to properly explore all the rooms and corridors here. And every room and every corridor was stuffed full of precious ornaments, sculptures, tapestries and paintings. There was so much gold in the Grand Hall alone that people had to shade their eyes when the sun shone down through the glass cupola.

As if the place didn't have enough treasure already, the powers that be down in London had apparently decided that a lot of the country's most valuable works of art should also be kept at Mentmore Towers for the duration of the War, it being considered that Rosebery's estate would be safely out of the way of the German bombers. And that surely was the case in Mary's experience; since the day she came, she hadn't heard or been told of a single bomb being dropped in the area. The works of art were stored in one of the outbuildings, known by everyone as "the refuge". It was rumoured that the golden coach used by the King during State ceremonies was also locked away in there, but since the refuge was guarded day and night, there was little chance of any of the staff seeing if that really was the case. Not for the first time during the present spell of freezing weather, Mary pitied the poor men who were outside doing the guarding.

Keen to hear Chaddie's "important announcement", the assembled staff not only finished their breakfasts quietly, but also did so quickly. There was an expectant hush when Chaddie rose from his seat again.

"Thank you. I won't keep you long," he began. "Can I ask you first of all not to waste your time repeating what I'm about to say to any of the staff not here at the table? Everyone will hear the news from me soon enough this morning.

"Now, as you'll all probably be aware, since his appointment a couple of years ago as Commissioner for Civil Defence in Scotland, His Lordship has been spending a lot of time north of the border on Government business. That has meant him making many trips up to Dalmeny House, his other home in Scotland, which some of us are very familiar with. Since he is always accompanied on his trips by Grace and I and a retinue of other key servants, together with all his and our goods and chattels, you'll appreciate that a great deal of organisation is needed every time. And that's not to mention the difficulties of the journey itself, which have been getting worse as the War has dragged on.

"So, last night His Lordship told me enough was enough. He has decided that he, the Countess and Lord Primrose will decamp to Dalmeny House until the War comes to an end and perhaps even after that. Naturally, he wants a good number of the staff, including Grace and I, to decamp with him."

Chaddie's audience was no longer quiet. Anxious conversations were breaking out up and down the table.

"Quiet now, please!" Chaddie shouted above the swelling talk. "Two things you should know right away. The first is that no-one will lose his or her job because of the move. A large number of staff will still be needed at Mentmore Towers to keep the house and the estate functioning. And, of course, we mustn't forget that we are also custodians of the nation's art treasures for the time being. For those reasons, probably about two-thirds of the present staff will remain here.

"As for the other one-third, the second thing to be aware of is that the move will be on a voluntary basis. I've managed to get His Lordship to agree that no-one will be *forced* to go up to Scotland. So what Grace and I intend to do over the coming days and weeks is to speak to each and every one of you to see where you stand. We can both testify that Dalmeny House is a beautiful country mansion in a beautiful setting on the shore of the River Forth. And we think the people most likely to want to live and work there are those without family or ties in this area."

Even before Chaddie finished the last sentence, Mary had known instinctively she would be going to Dalmeny House. She had seen a painting of the place in one of the drawing rooms, a grand old building surrounded by rolling green countryside. It reminded her very much of Castle Forbes in County Longford. The high flush now on her cheeks was caused not by her recent embarrassment, but by her excitement at the prospect of moving there – and living by the sea, something she had always dreamed of. She was also suddenly homesick. She wished that she could write to Aunt Bridget and tell her the latest news, but there was still an embargo on non-essential mail to and from Ireland. Her news would have to wait until after the War ended. *One day soon, perhaps,* she told herself.

1946
By the Sea

The servants' hall in Dalmeny House wasn't a hall at all, but a big alcove in the house's main kitchen. Inside it there was a long oak table, around which the staff could gather and eat. There was also a wireless in the corner, a grandfather clock against the wall, and above that those rows of little brass bells that governed a domestic servant's life by indicating, when rung, which of the multitude of rooms in the building required immediate service.

When she was on night duty, as she was now, Mary didn't mind sitting on her own in the alcove. It was so much cosier there than in that cold, draughty place they called the servant's hall down in Mentmore Towers. She usually passed the time by reading a book, but tonight she was otherwise occupied. Grace's sewing basket was open on the table in front of her. While listening to some dance band music on the Light Programme with one ear and keeping the other open for the tinkling of any of the brass bells, she was doing her best to darn two new rips in the already well-patched trousers of an old pair of pyjamas.

If a bell was to ring, Mary knew for certain it would be another summons to His Lordship's bedroom, where he would demand a fresh chamber pot. It was a nightly, sometimes twice-nightly, ritual. And all because the big, ugly brute was too lazy to walk the few steps to the water closet at the end of the corridor. At other times, the bell would go because he was after a glass of water. Mary wouldn't have been surprised if on one of those occasions he had also ordered her to read him a bedtime story and then tuck him in.

His Lordship's behaviour had been an eye-opener for Mary when she arrived at Dalmeny House and began working in her new position as upstairs maid. But nothing he did now shocked her – or even embarrassed her. It was his habit in the morning to climb out of his bath and walk buck naked and dripping wet from the bathroom back to his bedroom. It didn't seem to matter to him that any number of the maids might witness the sight of that big belly of his carried on those spindly legs as he squelched along the corridor, with his shrivelled-up manhood dangling for all to see. *He surely isn't proud to be showing off a body like that,* Mary thought at first, but then she realised he was simply demonstrating his utter disdain for the servants.

And Lord Primrose was happily following in his father's footsteps. Not for the first time had Mary and the other girls been woken from their sleep in the middle of the night by the noise of the shenanigans outside, and then watched from their rooms in the attic as Neil and his Hooray Henry pals, up from Oxford for the weekend, cavorted drunk and naked in the big fountain at the back of the house. To her, it was a case of the toffs drinking champagne and celebrating, as if the end of the War had suddenly set the world to rights, while the peasants continued to suffer rationing. The young Lord didn't have much in the way of manhood to be showing off either; perhaps it was something that ran in the family.

Mary had only one word to describe the way the two Lordships behaved – and that was arrogance. Every time she thought of the word, she also thought of Ireland and her father. It was the same arrogance of the British upper class that had ordered the execution of those poor, brave men who stood outside the General Post Office in Dublin on that fateful Easter Monday in 1916 and declared an Irish Republic. It was the same arrogance that led to her father and many other young men subsequently taking up arms against the British in Ireland's War of Independence. She could never forgive her father for abandoning his family, but she could understand now what drove him to join the IRA and how courageous he must have been. Whatever else, she would always be proud of him for that. Now that the

British Government didn't have a war to distract them, it was rumoured that they would soon agree to Ireland becoming a Republic, finally removing for all time her country's allegiance to the King. That would surely be a good thing for her father, and for all the other men and women, living and dead, who had fought for the cause.

The grandfather clock had begun to chime eleven o'clock when Mary halted her sewing to wonder how her father was doing. But it was only a fleeting thought. She was much more concerned about the other folk back home. She wanted to know about her mother and her brothers and sisters – and Aunt Bridget, of course. She had gone four long years with no news of them. Hopefully, though, a letter or two from home would arrive soon, now that the embargo on mail from Ireland had been lifted. She had sent a letter of her own to Aunt Bridget recently, telling her about the move up to Scotland and describing what a wonderful place she was living in.

Chaddie hadn't exaggerated back in Mentmore when he spoke about the Dalmeny Estate: Dalmeny House and its surroundings *were* truly beautiful. The house sat in the centre of a large landscaped park. There was an ancient woodland at the rear, while at the front, only a short walk away, was the estuary of the River Forth. It may not have been the *real* sea, but it was good enough for Mary, her only experience of the sea before then having been that terrible journey across the Irish one to England in what she could only describe as *an ould cattle boat*.

On her time off, she often wandered down to the water's edge and followed the shoreline to the west until she came to a headland. From up there, she could see what lay round the corner – and it was a breathtaking view. Down below was a long stretch of silvery sand, which the locals called the Shellbeds, then more woodland, and beyond that the magnificent orange-red structure of the Forth Bridge. It was said that the bridge was one of the modern Wonders of the World, and that surely was the case. The sight of it never failed to fascinate Mary, but at the same time it was oddly familiar, as if she had known it all her life.

The bridge lay some three miles away from Dalmeny House. The point where it began also marked the eastern edge of South Queensferry – the Ferry, as it was known locally. Everyone at the house referred to the place as a village, but in Mary's experience of villages in Ireland, the Ferry was much more of a town – and a busy one at that. At the Forth Bridge end, there was the Hawes Pier, from where a fleet of ferryboats sailed over to Fife and back all day, and next to it the famous Hawes Inn, in which she had once taken tea with Chaddie and Grace. At the other end, there was a big whisky distillery and along from that a naval dockyard, with much coming and going of ships from the Fleet. The Ferry also had its own picture house, which she had gone to several times with a few of the other maids. And, of course, she was familiar with the police station along there; "aliens" were still obliged to report their presence regularly, although she expected that requirement to be done away with any day now.

All in all, Mary thought the Ferry was a lively, magical place, full of history and character. But once again she had that feeling of having been there before. The Gypsies over in Ireland believed that people lived many lives; that when one life ended, it was only for another to begin. It was called reincarnation. Whether or not she had been reincarnated and had lived in the Ferry in the past, Mary thought it an awful pity to have waited so long in Mentmore Towers before she set foot in the place.

Having announced their intention to move to all the staff through Chaddie back in 1943, His Lordship and Her Ladyship proceeded to spend the best part of the next two years dithering about it, always believing that the War was due to end at any moment, thus removing the need for the move in the first place. When the War finally did come to an end in 1945, they immediately cancelled the move, but only to find out days later that the Earl had been appointed by Churchill as the Secretary of State for Scotland in the temporary Government he had formed pending a General Election. Then, of course, it was a case of flitting up to Scotland in all haste. By that time, the whole business had driven poor Chaddie demented.

But the last laugh occurred barely two months later, when the Election results were announced and the Labour landslide put Churchill and all his cronies, including the bold Earl, out of Government. Even Chaddie cracked a smile when he heard the news. Scottish Secretary or not, however, His Lordship made it clear that, having gone to all the trouble of moving to Dalmeny House, he and Her Ladyship were damned well there to stay now.

Still, though, there was a positive side to living at Mentmore Towers when the War ended, and that was being able to take part in the VE Day celebrations. A whole bevy of the staff travelled down to London for the event. It was a day Mary would never forget. There were crowds of people she would never see the like of again. All that singing and dancing – and all the drinking. They plied here with gin at one point, and before she knew it the "alien" was on top of a table dancing an Irish jig. She didn't remember much beyond that, but she vowed afterwards that it would be a cold day in hell before gin passed her lips again.

Mary was still reflecting on that momentous day in London when a voice in the alcove suddenly exclaimed, "Och, Jesus Christ, Mary, yer no' huvin' tae sew the miserable auld bastart's jama breeks again, ur ye?"

Mary looked up at the owner of the voice and smiled. "I am that, Jean," she replied. "His Lordship flung them at me earlier on. *Patch these properly this time*, he says. You know, with all the money he has, he could easily afford to put on a brand new pair of pyjamas every night for the rest of his life."

"Aye, he could–" Jean began, but stopped when one of the bells rang – angrily, it seemed. It was, as Mary had predicted, a summons to go to His Lordship's bedroom.

"You stay there, hen," Jean put up her hand. "Ah'll go an' attend tae the lazy auld skinflint. Ah'll gie him his piss pot, dinnae worry, an' pour the full yin right ower his fuckin' heid. Och, if only Ah could."

Jean left the alcove, but returned seconds later. "Christ, Ah near forgot, hen," she said. "Saturday night. There's a big dance bein' organised at the Rosebery Hall–"

Mary had looked puzzled at the mention of the Earl's name.

"The Toon Hall," explained Jean. "Aye, they named it efter the big bastart – or his faither, wan o' the two. Anyways, the dance is bein' held tae welcome aw the local lads returnin' frae the Forces. They're pittin' oan a really guid band, so Ah'm telt. There's a crowd o' us lassies frae the hoose goin'. You should come as well. Get ye oot o' yer shell an' introduce ye tae aw the local boys in their demob suits. But there'll still be plenty o' matelots aroond, if ye prefer the uniform. Either way, ye'll maybe find yersel' a guid man."

"Saturday, you say?" Mary smiled at Jean again. "Sure, I'll think about it." Then Jean was gone.

Mary and Jean were both upstairs maids in their early twenties. But there the similarities ended. Jean was a tall, red-haired Glaswegian who had worked at Dalmeny House for several years before Mary arrived. She was also much rougher than Mary, who still hadn't gotten used to her accent and the blasphemy; in fact, Jean reminded her a lot of those Dublin girls in the nuns' home back in Newtownforbes all those years ago. Rough or not, though, Mary liked Jean. Apart from Chaddie and Grace, she was probably Mary's only true friend in Dalmeny House.

As for the dance, well, perhaps she should go and *get oot o' her shell*, as Jean suggested. She had spent too long breaking her heart over Steve. Maybe it was high time she moved on. Steve had been one of the chauffeurs at Mentmore Towers. He was a few years older than her and very handsome, especially in his grey uniform. For several months, she and Steve had been– Now, how had Grace put it? Yes, *stepping out*. But then the War caught up with the poor boy. The conscription letter came, and off he went. The last she had heard he was over in Normandy with the landings. Then nothing. She had waited and waited for news, not knowing whether he was alive or dead. She kept a photograph of him under her pillow and looked at it every night before she went to sleep, sometimes crying herself to sleep. But now she should face up to the fact that she was never going to hear from him. She should go out and find herself another *guid man*.

1948
Derry

Hope View was a fitting name for the grand house at the top of The Loan in South Queensferry, it being occupied by the Very Reverend Canon Bernard O'Hanlon, who was the anointed shepherd of the Roman Catholic flock in and around the Ferry and whose fervent hope was to see the size of that flock multiply during his tenure. The house did indeed command a striking view of the River Forth, the world-famous bridge that straddled the river, and the green strip of the Fife coastline beyond. But well before that panorama it looked down imperiously on the Protestant church across the road and then on the sprawling whisky distillery towards the foot of the steep brae. Often of an evening, while his housekeeper cleared away the dinner dishes, Canon O'Hanlon stood at his dining room window, regarding those latter buildings. *Heathens!* he would mutter to himself when he thought of the congregation of St Andrew's, the parish church of the Church of Scotland. *Sinners!* he would also mutter when he reflected on the daily multitude of noisy distillery workers, only a handful of whom were part of his flock. Needless to say, *heathens* and *sinners* were his two favourite expressions.

The Chapel built next to *Hope View* was a less grand affair than the house itself and much less grand than St Andrew's down the hill. But St Margaret's Roman Catholic Church, to give the Chapel its proper name, was still big enough to accommodate Canon O'Hanlon's flock of some seven hundred saved souls. He had business in the vestibule of the Chapel this afternoon, business that would hopefully lead to a new family being brought into the fold.

"Now, my children," he was saying to the betrothed couple who sat across from him at the small table, on which the collection plates were placed during Mass times, "I'll be more than delighted to marry you later this year, but, as you know, there are some conditions that must be met before the marriage can take place."

Before proceeding, he examined the expectant faces of the two young people. There was Mary, a mere slip of a girl who worked as a maid for Lord Rosebery and who sounded as if she was fresh off the boat from Ireland. A pretty lassie, to boot. He was confident that, being Irish, she would understand and readily agree to the demands he was about to make.

But there was also Derry. Derry McKay. Not long released from his service in the Navy and, like many of the young men returning from the War, desperate to marry his sweetheart and make up for lost time. The problem was that the silver-haired priest knew the McKays. He knew Derry's grandfather and grandmother, in particular; sadly, more by repute than as faithful members of the flock. Those two were part of the mob of hard-drinking heathens and sinners who resided in that den of iniquity known as the Crossroads, the cluster of houses that was built by the Council on the edge of the town after the Great War and that was only a short walk down the hill from where he sat now. The only time any of that mob saw the inside of the Chapel was when they attended funerals and weddings. He didn't want Derry becoming one of them. There was time to save him. It was his duty to save the laddie's soul.

"You were both born into the Roman Catholic faith," he resumed. "That is an excellent start. But I do believe you are *lapsed* Catholics. Before I agree to wed you in here, each of you will have to prove to me beforehand that you are capable of *practising* the faith. By practising, I mean not only attending Mass every week, but also taking the Holy Sacrament. In addition, I need to be convinced that you will continue to practise the faith after the wedding. And remember, during the marriage ceremony you will be required to make a vow that your children will be brought up in the faith."

He paused again, this time to look directly at Mary.

"Now, my dear," he said, "you tell me that you've been working at Dalmeny House for a good while now, but I'm certain I've never seen you here at Mass. Unless you've been attending another church. In Edinburgh, perhaps?"

Mary blushed and shook her head. Then she tried to explain. "Well, no, Father. You see, it's difficult–"

"There can be no excuses for not attending Mass, girl," O'Hanlon snapped. "I hear Confessions on Wednesday mornings, Saturday mornings and Saturday evenings. And I conduct Mass on Sunday evenings, as well as twice on Sunday mornings. So you have plenty of opportunities to come. You will just have to make the effort, you hear me?"

From her time as a child in Carrigallen, Mary knew how to face up to belligerent priests. She had no fear of this particular one. But she desperately wanted to marry Derry, so she bowed her head, as if in submission, and murmured, "Yes, Father."

Satisfied with the response, O'Hanlon turned his attention to Derry. "And you, my boy. Prior to your War service, I doubt if you were ever familiar with this place. But will you now agree to become a good, practising Catholic? Making your Confession, then attending Mass and taking Holy Communion, all at least once a week?"

"Och, aye, Father," Derry grinned, "nae bother at aw. And I jist live doon the road."

Mary was watching Derry. That grin of his. The lopsided grin. That's what she loved most about him. That and his endless cheeriness, always whistling happily or singing to himself, no matter what. She first met him about a year before at one of those dances in the Rosebery Hall. She had been going to the dancing regularly with Jean and the other maids, but had never met anyone whom she actually liked, certainly no-one to compare with Steve. Then Derry appeared in front of her. With that grin. He was up in the Ferry on leave from Chatham Barracks, where he had been waiting to receive the official order for his release from the Navy, so he was still in uniform and looking like Fred Astaire in *Follow the Fleet*. And he was ever so polite.

"I'm sorry tae be so forward, miss," he had smiled at her with those twinkling dark eyes of his, "but I couldnae help noticin' you fae across the floor, and I wondered if you would care tae dance wi' me?"

How could she refuse such an invitation? "Yes, I'd love to," she had replied shyly. "But I have to warn you that I don't dance very well."

"Dinnae worry aboot that, miss. You jist follow ma lead and we'll be hunky-dory, you'll see."

And so they were. Not only did Derry look like Fred Astaire, but he also danced like Fred. Mary was literally swept off her feet. They stayed up on the dance floor all night. Afterwards, Derry walked her home, all the way to Dalmeny House in the dark. During that walk, he told her everything about himself. His full name was Charles Frederick Gisby, but, like her, he was called by his middle name, the Frederick being shortened to Derry. His father, Tom Gisby, came from England and was also in the Navy. But Tom's marriage to Derry's mother, Annie, didn't last very long, and Annie returned to live in the Ferry, where she remarried and had two more children. For most of his life, Derry stayed with his grandparents, Dan and Kate McKay, which was why everyone in the Ferry knew him as McKay, rather than Gisby.

For Mary, that had been a lot to take in during a first meeting, but she found it so easy to listen to Derry's soft, gentle voice. It was as if she had known him for a long time. She also learned that he was about a year younger than her. He had enlisted in the Navy as soon as he was old enough. By the time he went to sea, though, the War was all but done. He served on the aircraft carrier, *HMS Vengeance*, and sailed halfway round the world on her to places like Singapore and Australia – and Japan after the Atom Bomb was dropped on the country. He said he hadn't seen any action. Then it was shore barracks in England to bide his time along with all the other hundreds of thousands of men awaiting demobilisation.

Derry returned to Chatham the next day, promising Mary that he would see her again as soon as he was back in the Ferry. She didn't have long to wait. He was demobilised at the end of January, since when the pair of them had been together at every opportunity. She had introduced him to Chaddie and Grace, who took to him as if he was their long-lost son. They were also both very much in favour of "our young Mary" marrying such a gentleman. Knowing that Derry and Mary wouldn't be able to afford one otherwise, Grace had even promised to take Mary into Edinburgh and buy her the best wedding dress the city had to offer. And Derry's many relations in the Ferry were rallying round to pay for the reception. If all went well, the wedding would take place in September.

For Mary, it was all like a fairy-tale. She could hardly wait until September. She didn't know where they would be living or what they would be doing, and they likely wouldn't have two farthings to their name, but she would be with Derry, the man she loved, the perfect man. Neither could she wait to be out of Dalmeny House for good. She would miss Chaddie and Grace, of course, and some of the other staff, but she would be well rid of their two Lordships: Rosebery, the brute of a man she had to pander to every night, and Primrose – she had taken to calling him *the chinless wonder* – who was becoming more like his father every day.

Come September, Mary was also looking forward to becoming a part of Derry's family, whom she knew well by now. There was Annie, a small, friendly woman, who adored Derry. There was her husband, Cherry Quigley, a lovely, cheery fella Mary would be happy to call father. Then there were their two children, Derry's stepsister Catherine and stepbrother John. And finally there were Dan and Kate, Derry's grandparents. Dan was a bad-tempered, sour, old man, whom Mary couldn't abide, but she had a lot of time for Kate. That poor woman was old before her time. She had clearly lived a hard life, made even harder by the recent loss of her son, Jock, who was killed in Normandy during the D-Day landings. She was a feisty biddy, though, a bit of a legend in the Ferry. There was that story Derry told about the time his ship visited Perth in Australia. He met an older sailor, an Australian, in a bar. The man asked him whereabout in Scotland he came from.

"Edinburgh," Derry had replied, presuming that the man would never have heard of the Ferry.

"Hell, mate," said the man, "I was based not far from Edinburgh for a spell during the War. At the Port Edgar naval base. There's a little village just next to the base by the name of Queensferry. A real friendly place. I met this wonderful, old lady there. She made us all welcome. The life and soul of the party, mate. She was called Kate... Kate McKay. A wonderful lady."

Kate was a legend, true enough. She and Dan and the rest of the family lived in the Crossroads. Mary thought that they and the many other relations she was introduced to down there were a rough and ready lot, which was no bad thing as far as she was concerned, although it did have her wondering where Derry's politeness and gentleness came from; his real father, perhaps. She also wondered about the names of the people she met. As well as the McKays and Quigleys, there were any number of Hoggs and Mawdsleys and Bryants. All old Irish names. Second and third generation Irish, of course, but Irish nevertheless. Sure 'n' a visit to the Crossroads was for her like stepping into Little Ireland!

Getting to know Derry's family and all those other folk with their Irish names did make Mary homesick from time to time, especially for her brothers and sisters. She and Aunt Bridget were writing to each other every other week, so she was receiving regular bulletins from home – and the news was all good for the moment. With Ireland having become a proper Republic at last, owing no more allegiance to the British Government or the British Crown, both John and Michael had joined the legitimate Irish Army; they were *real* Irish soldiers now, and Mary was so proud of them. Thankfully, Joseph hadn't been enticed into becoming a priest; to think of him turning into one like the tyrant sitting across from her today – well, it didn't bear thinking about! As for Brendan and her three sisters, they were all "doing fine", according to Aunt Bridget. All that she could glean from Aunt Bridget about her mother was that the poor woman was still being cared for in a "sanatorium" somewhere near Dublin. And her father? Still drinking, apparently, but back living in his home village of Moyne.

Mary had written to Aunt Bridget to tell her about Derry, of course. But she didn't dare also mention the forthcoming wedding, at least not till it was over and done with. She simply didn't want her father catching a whiff of it and turning up in the Ferry, drunk as a lord and singing about *the bold Fenian men* – even if it was to the town's Irish diaspora. Besides, she was still officially an orphan. That's what would be recorded on the marriage certificate. And that's how it would have to stay for the time being. Even Derry wouldn't know the truth until she was ready to tell him. But that was for the future. First, the two of them had to convince this bully of a priest that they would become "good, practising Catholics".

Canon O'Hanlon was up on his feet now, rubbing his hands together and bringing the meeting to an end.

"All right, children, you both know what is required of you. We'll see how it progresses. In the meantime, that date in September for the wedding will remain in the diary. God go with you."

"Thank you, Father," Mary and Derry replied in unison.

"Thank Christ that's over," Derry said as soon as they were outside.

"Shoosh now, Derry," Mary whispered, linking Derry's arm with hers. "Blaspheming. And not even out of the Chapel grounds yet.

"Anyway," she continued as they climbed the steps and walked out of the Chapel gates, "it's not over. It's only just started. We'll be back here on Saturday for Confession, remember."

"Och, aye, so we will, hen," Derry laughed.

Mary pulled him closer to herself and laughed as well. Then they set off down the hill to Little Ireland.

1952

The First Children

It was the time of the Great Baby Boom. In the years immediately following the end of the Second World War, it seemed that all the young men and women throughout the United Kingdom wanted to marry, settle down and have children. As one historian described it, *The cry of the baby was heard across the land.* By 1952, Mary and Derry had made their own substantial contribution to that boom, having become the proud parents of three daughters and a son.

Hand-in-hand with the boom came a surge in the demand for housing from the new families, which in turn resulted in a severe shortage of suitable accommodation in towns and villages everywhere. The shortage was no less severe in South Queensferry. It was certainly severe enough for Mary and Derry to spend most of the first two years of their marriage living in Edinburgh. They did stay initially in Annie and Cherry's house in the Crossroads, but, with them and four other adults sharing that small house, conditions were cramped, to say the least. Mary and Derry craved a space of their own and the privacy that went with it, so the Capital it was. It was there that they had their first child, a daughter named Ann Marie. A son named Brendan followed about a year later.

The wheels of Government creaked slowly throughout those early post-War years; they were slow to recognise the housing problem and even slower to respond to it. By the time Brendan was born, however, major building programmes to supply new houses were underway by Councils up and down the land. In the Ferry, hundreds of Council houses for local people were to be built up at the back of the town on land that was purchased from Lord Rosebery. In allocating the houses, the Council would give priority to families who had had to move away from the Ferry because of the housing shortage, but even higher priority would go to families actually living in the town. It was because of the latter that Mary and Derry returned to the Ferry in 1950. Instead of living with Annie and Cherry again, they were able this time to obtain a flat in the notorious row of privately rented tenements known as Clark Place.

Built in the previous century for the better off artisans of the Ferry, the buildings in Clark Place had obviously seen better days. They had been allowed to deteriorate over the years and were now in a very poor condition. According to Mary, the place was little better than a slum. It was riddled with dampness. There were wash-houses at the foot of each tenement stair, but they were always flooded. Because there was no drying green, she and the other women had to string clotheslines from the downpipes at the front of the buildings across the road to the top of a wall opposite. And she swore that in her bed at night she could hear rats gnawing in the walls.

The "flat" that she and Derry rented was little more than a room and kitchen with a bed recess. Located at the rear of one of the tenements, it backed onto the goods yard of the distillery. After a major fire in 1949, the distillery was in the process of being rebuilt during all the time they stayed there, with all the noise that entailed. And if that wasn't enough, running through the goods yard was a railway line, which a deafening steam engine crossed and re-crossed day in and day out. While Mary could suffer the noise, the damp, the lack of space and even the rats, the single aspect of Clark Place that she abhorred most was having to share a lavatory with other families, some of whom she was often heard to tell Derry were no better than "filthy, dirty pigs".

But despite everything that she and Derry had to put up with in the place, they managed to add two more daughters to their growing family while they were there. Helena was born in the previous year and Mary only two months ago in the present year. They now had two babies and two toddlers to bring up in those awful living conditions. All four children were strong and healthy, though, thanks in no small part to the help that was provided by the midwives and nurses of the recently introduced National Health Service.

Throughout the two years they had spent so far in Clark Place, they expected at any moment to hear from the Council about the house they had applied for. It was a matter of waiting and waiting and waiting. And while they waited, circulating daily in the stairs and wash-houses were stories of families elsewhere in the Ferry – better off families living in more fortunate conditions – being allocated brand new homes.

"The hooses are goin' tae them an' such as them," the gossipers said. "It's a case o' who ye ken in the Ferry that'll get ye a hoose."

Being an incomer to the Ferry, Mary didn't know if any of these allegations were true. But then the stories began to take a more sinister tone. Her fellow-Catholic neighbours voiced suspicions that the freemasons were somehow manipulating the housing allocations to ensure that priority was given to Protestant families. Until she and Derry returned to live in the Ferry, Mary had never encountered religious bigotry; there was none in Ireland, of course, nor in the cossetted world of the Earl of Rosebery's estates. She hadn't even heard of the freemasons. But when Derry explained to her that it was a secret society, whose members controlled who received what jobs in both the dockyard and the distillery, the two main places of employment in the Ferry, with the lowest paid jobs always going to Catholics, she immediately likened them to the Pope-hating Orangemen who controlled the Six Counties that were annexed from Ireland. And she realised it was because of the freemasons that the best employment Derry was able to find in the Ferry was labouring work in the dockyard.

Mary couldn't believe that these same people also had a hand in deciding the housing allocations. Surely the Council was above that sort of thing. She didn't know, but she was determined to find out. She and Derry had waited long enough. It was high time she spoke to the man in charge, to hear an explanation straight from the horse's mouth. It was that quest which had brought her this afternoon to the Burgh Chambers of the Royal Burgh of South Queensferry, the grand building that sat prominently on its own at the east end of the High Street.

Along with several other Ferry women who were on the same quest, Mary sat on a bench in the ground floor hallway of the building, waiting her turn to see Mr Thomas Proudfoot, Burgh Surveyor. His name and job title were stencilled in gold leaf on the oak-panelled door opposite the bench. She was told that some women had gone there to shout the odds at Mr Proudfoot – or had sent their men down to do that. Whether that sort of behaviour had helped them obtain a house quicker, she had no idea. But it certainly wasn't part of her plan today. Rather than shout the odds at him, she aimed to charm the man. She had charmed earls and countesses – the Granards and Roseberys – hadn't she? The Roseberys had thought so highly of her, they had even contributed to the cost of her wedding reception. No, she would use some soft Irish charm on this man. And she had dressed especially for that. It was almost the end of September, but still warm outside, so she had put on a bright yellow summer frock that hugged her waist (which had already returned to its normal tiny size after baby Mary's birth in July) and a pair of white open-toed heels. With that get-up, a freshly powdered face and just a hint of lipstick, she was the Ferry's answer to Audrey Hepburn.

Presently, the Burgh Surveyor's latest visitor left his office. Then Mr Proudfoot himself appeared in the doorway. He was a stuffy-looking man, probably in his forties, although he looked older than that in his tweed jacket and flannels. He also wore one of those ridiculous pencil moustaches, and he had a pipe sticking out of the corner of his mouth.

He scanned the row of women on the bench. "Mrs… em… Jisby?" he asked.

"Gisby," Mary corrected him as she stood up, smiled and patted down her frock. Then, heels clacking, she sashayed through the door he held open for her.

"Please have a seat," he said, indicating the chair opposite his desk.

While he closed the door and walked to his own seat on the other side of his desk, Mary sat down and looked round the Burgh Surveyor's spacious office, which was located at the front of the building and had a large bay window looking out onto the High Street.

Mr Proudfoot picked up a single sheet of paper from his desk, read it quickly and put it down again.

"Now, Mrs... em..." he began,

"Gisby."

"Aye. So you're living at Clark Place just now wi' a husband and four children. Is that correct?"

"It is, Mr Proudfoot," Mary smiled as demurely as she could.

"And what can I dae for you the day, Mrs... em ...?"

"Gisby."

"Aye."

There was a pause. Mary put her hand to her mouth, politely cleared her throat and smiled again.

"Well, Mr Proudfoot, if I can just begin by telling you about the intolerable conditions in Clark Place..."

And Mary went on to recite everything that was wrong with where she lived, together with all the reasons why her family should be re-housed as quickly as possible. Being careful to stress that the suggestion came from other people and not her, she also hinted at the possible operation of religious discrimination in the way the new houses were being allocated.

While Mary spoke, Mr Proudfoot sucked on his unlit pipe and listened intently. But he wasn't listening to the words; he had heard them all before from the procession of women who had visited his office over many months. He was listening to the lilt in Mary's voice – that wonderful, magical Irish lilt. And he was drinking in the fresh, natural beauty of the colleen who owned the lilt. He wondered how she had managed to stay so slim and attractive after having four children. His own wife had given birth to just one brat and then turned into a dumpling.

Suddenly, the room was silent. It took him some seconds to realise that the woman had stopped speaking. He made a show of searching among the papers on his desk, but in reality he was trying to decide what to do next. Then, as if on impulse, he rose quickly from his chair and said, "Come ower tae the table, Mrs Jisby, and we'll see what can be done."

Mary followed him to the long table at the bay window, on which was spread out a plan of the Ferry's new housing scheme. All she could see was row upon row of little boxes. Most of the boxes were in blocks of four or more. Most were also shaded in a variety of colours.

"Have you heard o' the Scottish Special Housing Association, Mrs Jisby? The SSHA?"

"No, I don't think so."

"Well, they're a Government agency who are helping Cooncils across Scotland wi' their building programmes. And they're helping us oot here in the Ferry. Now, see the hooses here that havnae been shaded in? They're in Rosebery Avenue–"

"Jesus, they haven't named a street after the ould bugger?"

Mary instantly regretted her outburst, but Mr Proudfoot laughed out loud.

"I'm afraid so," he said.

He liked this woman. If only he had been twenty years younger. And that perfume she was wearing was so intoxicating. He didn't know, of course, that the scent was of cheap lavender water, which was all that Mary could afford.

"Anyway, these hooses are due tae be built by the SSHA," he continued. "They'll be using a brand new building technique called no-fines concrete. The walls are made in a factory across in Sweden, wi' concrete poured into moulds, and then shipped ower here–"

"A prefab!" Mary looked aghast. "I can't be doing with a prefab, Mr Proudfoot, not with four child–"

"Naw, naw, Mrs Jisby, they're no' building prefabs. They'll be building proper hooses wi' proper walls. The only reason I'm telling you aboot the no-fines method is tae explain that these hooses will be built much quicker than the Cooncil could do. We could have your family in yin o' them inside aboot a year, maybe a wee bit longer than that. You can take your pick o' them right noo the day. Any o' the unshaded yins."

Mary brightened up and eagerly examined the plan. She spotted a block of only two boxes towards the end of Rosebery Avenue on the left.

"What's that?" she asked, pointing at the block.

"Aye, they're what we call semi-detached hooses. There's no' many o' them in the scheme. Both o' them will have three bedrooms, so either yin wid suit you. You jist choose which."

Mary didn't know why, but she decided on the house on the right-hand side of the block. Its box was marked 48. She placed the tip of her finger on it.

"That one," she said.

"Number 48?"

"Number 48, yes."

Mary's cheeks were glowing from excitement. Forty-eight would be her lucky number from now on, she decided. She had been married in 1948. It was a good number.

Taking the pipe out of his mouth for the first time, Mr Proudfoot nodded at Mary. He looked and sounded pleased with himself.

"Right, noo, Mrs Jisby, let's gang back ower to ma desk tae dae the paperwork."

Mary began to follow him, but stopped when she remembered.

"Sorry, Mr Proudfoot, but I wonder if you could tell me what this line on the map means?"

She indicated the narrow green strip running all along Rosebery Avenue between the pavement in front of the houses and the road.

"Och, that? That wis the architect's idea tae have a grass verge for the Cooncil tae plant trees in. Make it a proper avenue. A boulevard," he added, laughing.

But just the thought of living in a tree-lined avenue had Mary in seventh heaven.

Less than ten minutes later, paperwork completed, Mary came out of the Burgh Chambers, click-clacking down the steps into the late afternoon sunshine. There was a big grin across her face. *Mission accomplished*, she said to herself.

1954

The New House

Now that it was safe to do so, Kate McKay let go of the hands of her two greatgrandchildren and fished inside a pocket of her coat. Pulling out a crumpled handkerchief, she used it to wipe her nose, which had been streaming in the bitter January air. Then she blew her nose into it, making a loud raspberry noise that caused the other two bairns facing each other in the pram to giggle.

"That's some trek tae get here fae doon the Ferry, Mary," she said. "Ah'm fair pechin' noo, hen."

"I dare say we'll all get used to it, Kate," replied Mary as she wheeled the pram sideways in front of her so that she could keep an eye on both Helena and baby Mary while she also took a good look at the house.

She and Kate and the four children were on the as yet untarmacked pavement directly in front of Number 48 Rosebery Avenue. Pushing the pram all the way up from Clark Place to there hadn't phased Mary at all. She may have given the impression of a petite, fragile young lady, but she was as strong as an ox. With all the heavy work she had had to do over the years, first at home in Carrigallen, then for the nuns in their laundry room, and latterly in Aunt Bridget's smallholding, she needed to be strong.

So if Mary was out of breath like Kate, it wasn't from the walk up; it was much more to do with her excitement at seeing that the house was almost finished. Even the front door had been painted and its number screwed on. But with a lavatory pan and a cistern sitting outside the house, and outside each of the other houses being built by the SSHA, it was clear that the plumbing work still hadn't been completed. Nevertheless, it looked like they would be able to move in soon now. The house would be ready quite a bit later than promised by Mr Proudfoot, which meant that they were having to endure another winter in cold, damp Clark Place. But late or not, it was just as well, because she had recently found out that she was pregnant again.

"Don't you be wandering too far away," Mary called to Ann Marie. "And you, you wee eejit, get your head out of there," she shouted at Brendan, who was attempting to copy the workman he had seen spitting into one of the lavatory pans further along the road.

"Dinnae worry, hen, I'll keep a guid watch oan the pair o' them," said Kate. "You jist dae whit you came tae dae. My, but it's a braw hoose," she added.

Mary nodded at Kate, thinking that there in the brightness of the winter's day the old woman looked every one of her seventy-one years and more besides. Since Dan McKay's death about eighteen months ago, Kate's body had grown thinner and more stooped, and her face more lined. It was the opinion of everyone who knew Dan that Kate would be better off not having to live with that sick, cantankerous, wicked man, but Kate seemed to be lonely without him. All the same, she carried on with her routine, still smoking her ten Woodbines and drinking her gill of whisky a day, and still delivering the newspapers round the Crossroads. And most lunchtimes she was still to be found in the public bar of the Queensferry Arms Hotel, sitting with her cronies and reminiscing on the good old days in the Ferry.

In the same period since Dan's death, a bond had formed between Kate and Mary, perhaps because of Mary's closeness to Derry, the grandson Kate had raised as if he was her own son. Kate became a frequent visitor to Clark Place, where she took the older children off Mary's hands for a spell or sat with the younger ones, "diddlin' ma greatgrandbairns on ma knee", as she described it. And today she had offered to accompany Mary and the children on the walk to Rosebery Avenue.

"It surely is a braw house, Kate," Mary murmured.

So, while Kate lit a cigarette and watched Ann Marie and Brendan as they explored the tarpaulins and piles of bricks and other paraphernalia left by the builders, and while Helena and baby Mary took in the unfamiliar surroundings, Mary returned to her examination of their future home.

From the drawings shown to her and Derry by the SSHA housing officer who came to see them before Christmas, she had memorised the internal layout of the house. There were three bedrooms upstairs: a big one at the back and two smaller ones at the front, both of which they were told would have views of the Forth Bridge. Downstairs, there was the hall, a living-room, a big kitchen and a bathroom. *Our very own bathroom with an actual bath after all this time!* she exclaimed to herself. There would also be hot water from a boiler heated by the coal fire in the living-room or by an immersion heater when they didn't light the fire in the summer. *Jesus, didn't I have to show my ignorance and ask the housing officer what an immersion heater was?* As well as a gas cooker in the kitchen, there would be a gas-heated boiler for washing clothes, a miniature version of the one she had to sweat over for the nuns back in Newtownforbes. And apparently there was a big, deep cupboard at the back of the house for storing coal. *Dear Lord, a coal cellar in the house – who'd have believed it!*

Mary sighed. The house had everything. It was a dream come true. But there were so many practical things to think about before they moved in. Things like proper beds and bedding, furniture, carpets, crockery for the kitchen, and pots and pans, and likely much more. There was little enough to bring with them from Clark Place, so it would all have to be paid for with money they didn't have. There was the new baby to think about as well, another mouth to feed.

She sighed again. She would worry about all those things on another day. Right now, she wanted to savour the moment, to imagine what their new life would be like. So she closed her eyes and took a deep breath. The air felt so fresh, as if they were in the middle of the countryside. Just up the hill, running parallel with Rosebery Avenue, there was another road called

Dundas Avenue, named after another toff, where new houses were also being built. But beyond Dundas Avenue there was field upon field for many miles. They actually *were* in the countryside up there. Derry had said that there was a small wood at the end of Rosebery Avenue, with a path running through it to a farmer's track which led to the village of Dalmeny and which the locals called Lovers' Lane. Mary could picture Derry and her and the children strolling along Lovers' Lane of a summer's evening. It was a blissful picture.

But she mustn't forget their garden. They would have plenty of it at the front and back of the house, as well as along the side. At the back, which was south-facing, she wanted a proper drying green, of course, and enough space left for growing potatoes and vegetables, and for planting gooseberry and blackcurrant bushes so she could make jam like her mother used to before the poor woman fell ill. Down the side, they would have shrubs – rhododendrons and such like. The front garden would be special, though, full of brightly coloured meadow flowers, and with wild pink and white and yellow roses climbing all along the fence. It would remind her every day of the little garden they kept in Carrigallen. But without the chickens and Dev, the bad-tempered goat! Derry had said he was good at the gardening and could do all that for her.

And then, to add to their beautiful garden, there would be the trees to be planted in front of the house – along the strip of ground she was standing on right now. She wondered what kind of trees would be chosen. Cherry trees, perhaps, with their glorious pink blossom in the springtime, another reminder of back home. Or good old Scottish rowan trees, with their bright red berries in winter. Whatever trees were picked, Rosebery Avenue would be a wonderful place to live and a wonderful place to raise their children, however many they ended up with.

Yes, the children. She would do her damnedest to make sure they were brought up nothing like the Lanes of Carrigallen, with their raggedy clothes and dirty, bare feet. Her children would be the smartest and brightest and best dressed kids in the whole of the Ferry. That would be her mission in life. Ann Marie would be starting school after the summer. It was a pity that Canon O'Hanlon had only recently won his long battle with the Roman Catholic Church and the County Council – and, she had been told, certain quarters of the local community – to have a Catholic primary school provided in the Ferry. It would still be some years before it was built. In the meantime, Ann Marie would need to travel on the SMT bus to the nearest Catholic school in the County, which was in Winchburgh, about five miles away. Brendan and the other two girls would probably also have to go to Winchburgh at first, but soon enough the four children would be attending the new Ferry school, which would be just a short walk away down the road.

And when they were all at school and this latest one was born, she would see about getting a job. God knew that Derry worked hard to provide for all of them, but his wages were never going to be enough for a growing family and everything that needed to be bought for the new house. So she had to be working as well, if need be at night when Derry came home from the dockyard. Then, when they were both working, they might be able to scrape enough together to pay for her to travel to Ireland to see Aunt Bridget and her brothers and sisters – and perhaps even her mother – after all these years. She had heard that Aer Lingus would soon be flying out of Turnhouse Airport to Dublin, so she might be able to go over on the plane. *An ould cattle boat coming and a fancy aeroplane with shamrocks painted on it returning – that would surely be something!*

Mary closed her eyes again and took another deep breath. Oh, yes, life up there was going to be wonderful. It was never going to be easy, though. There was bound to be sadness mixed with the joy. There were bound to be money problems and health problems. But she would take them in her stride, just as she had done all her life. *Sure 'n' am I not the daughter of an ould Irish rebel?*

Epilogue

Helena Mary Bella Gisby (*née* Lane) lived at 48 Rosebery Avenue for the rest of her life. She was known to her neighbours and her neighbours' children, but especially the children, as a kind and generous person, a lady with a big heart. In keeping with the maxim of poor folk in rural Ireland at the time that you should share what little you have with those who are even poorer than you, no beggar, and there were many of them roaming the Scottish countryside in the 1950's and 1960's, was ever turned from her door without at least a coin or some food. In fact, it was said that secret signs had been laid by the itinerant people to point the way to her house.

Mary had three more children – Patricia in 1954, Bernadette in 1956 and Shaun in 1960 – to make a family of seven in all. But, as she had predicted, there were times of deep sadness in her life. Patricia died only nine months after being born. And Derry was to die in 1965 before he had reached the age of forty.

She did manage to return to Ireland twice, on both occasions flying on "a fancy aeroplane with shamrocks painted on it". The first time was to attend the funeral of her "ould rebel" of a father, who died alone in 1962 not long after receiving a medal and a war pension from the Irish Government in recognition of his service with the IRA during the War of Independence. The second occasion was a holiday in 1964, when she was to meet all her brothers and sisters, the mother hen reunited with her assorted chicks, as well as her beloved Aunt Bridget, who by that time was living in Dublin with her husband, a lovely man by the name of Benny Lynch.

No-one knows for sure, but it is highly unlikely that Mary ever saw her mother again after that fateful day in Carrigallen when she was sectioned and taken away to be incarcerated in a mental hospital. The woman died in 1972, still incarcerated.

As for Mary herself, her big heart finally stopped beating in 1984, shortly before her sixtieth birthday. Her six surviving children have collaborated to produce this book in her memory and to publish it in the centenary year of Ireland's Easter Rising of 1916, a momentous event, the telling of which was never far from their mother's lips.

Sadly, the Council never did plant those trees in the grass verge along Rosebery Avenue.

About the Author

Brendan Gisby was born in Edinburgh, Scotland, halfway through the 20th century, and was brought up just along the road in South Queensferry (the Ferry) in the shadow of the world-famous Forth Bridge. He is the author of several novels and biographies and a mountain of short stories. He is also the founder of **McStorytellers** (http://www.mcstorytellers.com), a website which showcases the work of Scottish-connected short story writers.

Printed in Great Britain
by Amazon